Houses

AN ARCHITECTURAL GUIDE

D1502111

Pevsner Introductions

Houses

AN ARCHITECTURAL GUIDE

Charles O'Brien

Yale University Press | New Haven and London

Pevsner Introductions draw extensively on the Pevsner Architectural Guides, the series founded by Sir Nikolaus Pevsner in 1951. Readers wishing to know more about the architecture of a particular area should consult the relevant **Buildings of England** volume. There are also companion series for the **Buildings of Ireland**, **Scotland** and **Wales**. Specialist terms given in small capitals in this text are explained in more detail in *Pevsner's Architectural Glossary*, available both in print and as an app.

YALE UNIVERSITY PRESS | NEW HAVEN AND LONDON
www.pevsner.co.uk   www.yalebooks.co.uk
www.lookingatbuildings.com   www.yalebooks.com

Designed by Catherine Bankhurst
Typeset in Johnston ITC Standard and Minion Pro
Printed in China

British Library Cataloguing in Publication Data
Data available
Library of Congress Cataloging in Publication Data
Data available

ISBN 9780300233421

Frontispiece: Kersey, Church Hill and The Street, Suffolk

Endpapers: Selected house plans from the Pevsner Architectural Guides

Contents

INTRODUCTION

Anyone picking up this book for the first time will have lived in at least one type of house or flat, and more if their place of education or work has occupied buildings that began as houses. The age and type of those buildings will vary greatly. England has a little over 22 million dwellings, of which about one-fifth were built before the end of the First World War; a slightly smaller proportion (about 16%) were built in the period from 1919 to 1945 alone. Well over half of the rest have been built between the end of the Second World War and 1990, and a much smaller proportion since that time. Of the entire housing stock, about 80% are houses (mostly two-storey) or bungalows and about 20% are flats. Some 220,000 houses are listed as of Special Architectural or Historic Interest.

This introduction is intended as a companion to the *Buildings of England* series of architectural guides launched in 1951 by Sir Nikolaus Pevsner. From the beginning of the series, each county guide has been accompanied by an introduction setting the buildings described in the gazetteer in the wider context of England's architectural history. This is the first attempt to draw together some of the principal themes of those introductions into a single introduction to houses, which after churches are the building type most heavily represented in the pages of the 'Pevsner Guides'. The main focus is on houses of the aristocratic level and below, but the more specialized types of residence such as castles and royal or ecclesiastical palaces are omitted. It is primarily an attempt to explain how the most common forms of dwelling to be discovered in English towns and villages have developed since the Anglo-Saxon period in response to the changing demands of their occupants and architectural fashion.

1. Budenberg Haus Projecte flats, Altrincham, Cheshire, by Foster & Partners, 2003–7

The book draws on nearly two decades of work for the Pevsner Architectural Guides. Those who write for the series must visit and describe hundreds of country houses, cottages, farmhouses, flats, bungalows and tower blocks in the course of their work. Few houses, even those of quite recent date, will be found unaltered since the day that their builders handed over to their occupants. In houses that have survived several centuries it can be expected that every generation will have had an impact upon their appearance, positively or otherwise. Unpicking the phases of their development is not easy without detailed records (a rarity even for some of the largest houses) and much must be done by examining the individual features and motifs to detect what they might tell us about how a house has grown (or shrunk) over time. Exteriors may be misleading and the face that a house shows to the world can prove no more than a façade when seen from the side or the back. Penetrating within may tell yet another story or multiple stories that change from one room to another. Walls, windows, doorcases, staircases may have moved or changed on one or more occasions, and even trying to determine a date on the basis of style may be risky, because later periods were often enthusiastic imitators of earlier ones. Even the confident house investigator should proceed with caution!

MEDIEVAL AND TUDOR HOUSES
TO 1540

The National Heritage List for England has nearly ten thousand records for houses that are medieval or partly medieval. For the early medieval period – broadly from the departure of the Romans in the early c5 until the Norman Conquest – although churches survive, there are no standing remains of Saxon settlers' houses. Excavation of their villages, however, has revealed enough to determine what they were made of and how they were used. At West Stow in Suffolk several houses have been reconstructed from evidence of the buildings which existed there in the c5–c7. Their form was very simple: a single hut, built of timber and covered by a thatched roof. The walls consisted of either rough planks or of wattle panels

2. West Stow, Suffolk. A recreated group of Saxon houses on the site of a village (occupied c. 420–650 A.D.) which was excavated between 1965 and 1972 and consisted of three or four groups of houses with a hall at the centre of each group

covered in daub. Families would have lived and slept in a single room. Some of these huts were sunk into the ground, possibly providing a rudimentary basement or cellar. The largest form of dwelling would have been the HALL, with a central hearth for the fire to heat the room and for cooking. This determined that the hall should be a tall room open to the roof to allow smoke to escape and to protect the roof itself from catching fire. Furnishings must have been simple and probably no more than wooden tables and benches and chests for storage. Nevertheless, even in this simple form we can recognize the essential features of a dwelling as we understand it today. These Saxon houses are the beginning of a continuous tradition in the development of houses over a thousand years.

Later Medieval Houses

The Norman Conquest heralded a transformative era in architecture, but among houses there is nothing comparable to the design revolution found in Norman religious and defensive buildings. Furthermore, with the exception of castles, hardly any houses or parts of houses have survived from before 1250 (but see also the Jew's House, Lincoln, p. 19).

The OPEN HALL was the predominant type of dwelling throughout the later medieval period (c12 to late c15), in which the main living and eating space was a single room, open to the roof and with a central fire for heating and cooking. In many houses this hall was also a place for sleeping. At the 'high' end of the hall would have been the table of the owner; the main entrance would have been on one side of the 'low' end. Frequently a corresponding door on the other side led from the rear of the house to outbuildings.

Wealthier owners made refinements and augmented the plan to provide a greater level of comfort. A significant development, for example, was the insertion of a SCREEN to form a through passage between the front and back doors and thus keep out draughts from the hall itself. From the mid c13 and especially after 1300 this basic rectangular plan evolved with the attachment of further rooms to the hall. Many houses were built with two service rooms at the low end – a buttery (for butts of wine and ale) and a pantry (for bread). Each would have a door opening directly from the hall – or within the screens passage – but there would frequently be a third door that led into a passage giving access to the kitchen, which was almost always contained in a separate building to avoid the risk of fire. At the same time, other rooms were provided as private quarters such as a parlour or bedchamber to which the owner could retire away from the rest of the household. To begin with such rooms might be set over the service rooms at the low end of the hall and be used for both sitting and sleeping, but as time passed it became more common, not least for reasons of convenience and privacy, to place these rooms at the high end of the hall with their own door.

3. Priest's House, Muchelney, Somerset. Built c. 1308, this displays all of the features that characterise the evolution of many houses from the C14–C16. The positions of the door and windows show that it has an open hall more or less in the centre, indicated by the large window, that its entrance is at the 'low' end with service rooms to its l. and to the r. of the hall the windows in two storeys show it has a parlour below a bedchamber. The designs of the windows show, however, that they are later than the building itself and such improvements are to be expected, as is the insertion of chimneys, which are an innovation of the C16

Building in this position also allowed construction of rooms on two storeys corresponding to the full height of the hall, with a storage room or parlour on the ground floor and a private chamber for the owner's family above. It is usual to refer to this upper room as the SOLAR and the part of the building in which it is contained as the solar tower (or chamber block): a good early surviving example is the Manor House at Boothby Pagnell, Lincolnshire, built *c.* 1200, although there the hall to which it was attached has been demolished, or the grander example of the late C13 Solar Tower at Stokesay Castle, Shropshire.

With this subdivision of the house it is common to describe medieval hall houses in terms of units. A single-unit house consists of just one room, two-unit houses a hall with adjoining room (usually for services) at one end, three-unit a hall with a room at each end, and so on. Even after halls had started to have additional bays for ancillary rooms, the entire range of functions in the stone or timber-framed house was often still contained within a rectangular plan, with a single roof covering all. In Cornwall, Devon and parts of northern England the characteristic form of houses is known for obvious reasons as a 'longhouse' and were designed to accommodate livestock in a byre or 'shippon' located beyond the entrance passage, in place of the service rooms more usually found there. Inhabitants and livestock shared a common entrance. This form of rural dwelling persisted well beyond the medieval period.

A change especially evident in the C14 and C15 is the development of separately roofed two-storey cross-wings, set at right angles to the hall at one or both ends and extended further out, allowing more space for the services and the chamber above. This created the familiar form of late medieval houses with an L-plan (cross-wing projecting at one end), T-plan (with cross-wing at one end projecting to front and rear; also called a single-ended hall); or H-plan, with two cross-wings projecting front and back (also sometimes called a double-ended hall), prevalent from the mid C14 onwards.

A well-known variant of the hall house with cross-wings is the WEALDEN HOUSE (*see* fig. 4c) dating from *c.* 1370 onwards and particularly prevalent in Kent, Surrey, Sussex, and parts of eastern

Hampshire – areas where yeoman farmers enjoyed significant prosperity in the later medieval period. Despite the name, examples have been discovered well into the Midlands of England and further north where they are more commonly found in towns. Such dwellings are easily identified by their distinctive front elevation, in which the upper floors of the wings project and carry the eaves of a roof – usually hipped (with sloping rather than gabled ends) – over the central hall, so the impression is of a recessed centre. In the towns, such houses might be built in a continuous row (e.g. Spon Street, Coventry).

Generally speaking, houses with cross-wings at both ends are likely to have been built for inhabitants socially superior to those living in L- or T-plan houses, while the grandest houses of the aristocracy between the c14 and mid c16 adopted a courtyard plan. This evolved as a means of accommodating all the functions and services of the largest households and the full complement of chapel, lodgings, stables, brewhouses and laundries. Such houses are in effect an extension of the standard three-unit hall house – which now formed one side of the court – but with cross-wings developed into side

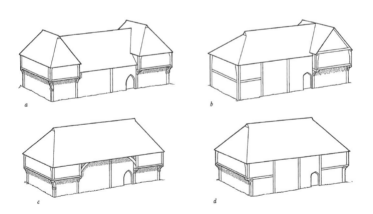

4. Some examples of medieval hall house types in Kent: a) Central hall with two-storey cross wings; b) Central hall with two-storey cross wing at 'low' end and solar at high end with hipped roof; c) Wealden house with central open hall; d) Two storey house with central open hall and end jetties to the wings

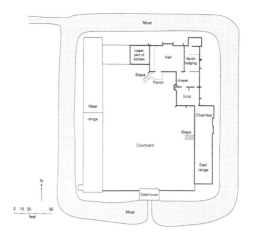

▲ 5. Markenfield Hall, Yorkshire West Riding. Built c. 1290–1310, plan. The arrangement of the buildings shows how the standard pattern of a hall house could be developed to provide more luxurious accommodation: here a chapel and the solar tower at right angles to the rest provided accommodation on two storeys. Courtyard plan houses with defensive purpose continued to be built longer in the north of England than elsewhere

▼ 6. Haddon Hall, Derbyshire. One of the best preserved medieval courtyard houses, developed from the C12 to the C16. To begin with it had a single courtyard (r.) with the hall at the centre of the rear range. The second (upper) court was added later and contained the most private apartments to which most visitors would not have been admitted

ranges linked by an outer range containing a gatehouse in line with the hall entrance. Some such houses might also have a defensive purpose. No man could build a defensive house in England without permission from the Crown, and the granting of a 'licence to crenellate' is often one of the first pieces of evidence to indicate a firm date for the building of a medieval house, even if the crenellation may be the finishing touch – in which case the licence date is that of completion rather than commencement. A good early example is Markenfield Hall, West Riding of Yorkshire, where the licence was granted in 1310 but the style of the tracery of the hall windows clearly indicates that it was begun *c*. 1290.

Markenfield has a single court protected by a moat, but over the course of the medieval period some of the grandest houses developed double, triple and even quadruple courtyards (e.g. Herstmonceux Castle, East Sussex, for which licence to crenellate was given in 1441). The Tudor courtyard houses are on a far grander scale than those of the late medieval period and those of the early C16 reached an extent previously unheard of, providing accommodation for households running into hundreds of people. Hampton Court, with its base or outer court, is the best preserved of the very grandest houses to adopt this form, but since this was the palace of Cardinal Wolsey and then the king it is hardly representative. Nevertheless the late C15 and early C16 produced many ambitious houses for the wealthiest patrons such as bishops and heads of monastic foundations but also increasingly those courtiers who were newly enriched by royal favour and from the 1530s the proceeds from the break-up of church estates at the Dissolution. They followed the king's lead in large building enterprises and often in the expectation of a royal visit. Cotehele, in Cornwall, is an excellent example of a house of *c*. 1520 built by Sir Richard Edgcumbe which still retains its outer, inner and service courtyards. This division represents the hierarchical arrangement of the largest households, progressing from lodgings for lesser servants and stabling for horses in the outer court and an adjunct to this being a kitchen court, to the inner court, where one side might be the domain of more important servants and another was taken up by the hall itself.

▲ 7. Lower Brockhampton House, Brockhampton-by-Bromyard, Herefordshire. A moated house of c. 1400, with gatehouse of c. 1542–3. The fact that
the gatehouse is so much later than the house indicates the importance of
this feature as a status symbol for the owner of even quite modest houses.
The house itself had its hall in the l. range and service rooms in the wing.
Inside the screens passage are still three doors to the buttery, pantry and
kitchen

    In courtyard houses a moat gave a measure of protection from the
outside world and this was reinforced by a gatehouse that allowed
control over those visiting the house, monitored by the porter, who
was lodged within it. In houses with an outer and inner court it was
not uncommon for the inner court to have its own gatehouse. The
most lavish gatehouses are associated with aristocratic, episcopal
and monastic residences, and are flanked by corner turrets to give
them special architectural emphasis. By the late c15 such gatehouses

8. Yanwath Hall, Cumbria. This has a complete solar tower of comfortable rooms on two storeys above a vaulted ground floor, built in the late C14 and C15 (the large windows with mullions are Elizabethan insertions made when the interiors were altered). The lower range adjoining was probably built in the C15. It contained the open hall, and the position of its 'high' end is clearly indicated by the projecting window with two tiers of windows with cusped heads. The porch marks the position of the entrance to the cross passage, beyond which is the kitchen, indicated by the prominent chimneys

in courtiers' houses are prodigiously high, and now more for show than protection, e.g. at Oxburgh Hall, Norfolk (1482), and this tradition of erecting dominant gatehouses runs through all of the largest Tudor mansions of the early–mid C16, such as Hampton Court or the house at Layer Marney, Essex (*see* p. 30). Of the same period, however, there are many modest examples, including the charming timber-framed gatehouse of 1542 straddling the moat of Lower Brockhampton House, Herefordshire.

As the medieval house plan developed and extended, the hall in the central range became a room reserved for entertainments and reception of guests. The day-to-day activities of the household now took place in the private apartments beyond the hall. The general trend in all but the largest houses, where the large open hall was a matter of prestige, was towards smaller halls and increased emphasis on the private wings. Ground-floor parlours were introduced in the cross-wings, with a withdrawing chamber above occupying the full depth of the cross-wing. In the largest houses there were suites of ever-more private chambers and in the later medieval period some of the previously separate buildings, such as kitchens, started to be integrated into the main structure of the house. Finally, from the late C15, the era of the open hall came to an end in most houses with the insertion of floors, confining the hall to the ground floor with an additional chamber above it.

Although open halls of the type described above account for the vast majority of medieval houses, there are some local variations. In some areas, especially Cumbria and Northumberland, some later medieval houses take the form of a tower of two or more storeys with a first-floor H A L L above a room either for storage or livestock; the hall was only accessible at first-floor level via from an external stair, providing a measure of protection. Alternatively such a tower, as at Yanwath Hall, Cumbria (*see* p. 17), which dates from the late C14, might provide an adjunct to a hall as well as a potential place of refuge. This tradition continued long after any defensive threat had receded. In Northumberland such houses, known as B A S T L E S, were being built well into the C17.

Town Houses

The types of medieval houses described so far are mostly found in rural or formerly rural areas. Town houses developed in different ways. Medieval towns were typically laid out with narrow plots of land running back for some length away from the street. These 'burgage plots' dictated the width of the houses. Most medieval town houses are of one of two kinds however varied in size. The first is a version of the typical rural house with the hall set parallel to the street, the entrance and services at the low end and a chamber at the high end. In the other type the hall stands at right angles to the street. In these examples, especially common in the busiest commercial areas of large towns, the end facing the street or marketplace might incorporate a shop or other commercial use on the ground floor, with the hall directly behind and the kitchen and other service areas beyond that. A third variation, and the grandest, is the courtyard plan where the hall might be placed at the rear of the court. Pressure for space commonly resulted in all living accommodation being kept to the first floor, leaving the entire ground floor for storage of goods etc. These might take the form of stone UNDER-CROFTS. Winchelsea, East Sussex, is one of the most famous examples of a town with numerous such cellars surviving below houses rebuilt at a later date. In the Rows at Chester the medieval houses are also built over vaulted store rooms at street level. Access to the

9. Jew's House, Lincoln. An early survival of a town house, its later C12 date clearly indicated by the Romanesque mouldings of the window arches at first floor. The hall and living accommodation were on the upper floor, leaving the ground floor for other uses, probably shops, and with an external staircase to reach the hall

▲   10. Watergate Street Row, Chester. This shows the first floor walkway serving the entrance to the shops and houses and covered by the upper chamber of the house. The hall was situated behind the shop and open to the roof

shops and dwellings is provided by a continuous walkway (the Row) at first floor. This manner of designing seems to have begun by the mid-c13 and is a unique variation on a more familiar medieval pattern of extending the first floor over the street as for example in Winchester's High Street. As demand in urban areas intensified the plots were subdivided, producing exceptionally narrow fronts and considerable buildings at the rear. The means of access to the rear parts, if not through the shop and house, often had to be by a passage along the side. Even where the houses have been refronted or rebuilt at a later date the existence of such passages is a clear indicator of their medieval origin.

Materials and structures

In large areas of England, houses built of stone, flint (in chalk areas) or river cobbles are the norm, because the materials were readily accessible. They employed large stones at the base and corners of the walls to give strength. In other areas the expense of extracting, transporting and dressing stone means that only the most prestigious medieval houses were constructed of this material. In the South-West COB was a popular material for walls. It is a compressed material formed of wet earth and straw which hardens on drying and is then protected from the weather by a layer of whitewash or other coating. Similar forms of walling in clay, mud or clay lump

▼ II. Winchester, Nos. 33 & 34 High Street, reconstruction, isometric drawing by Jonathan Snowdon

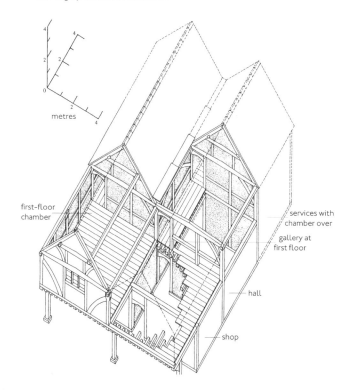

metres

first-floor chamber

services with chamber over

gallery at first floor

hall

shop

(specific to East Anglia) go by different names in other parts of the country (e.g. wychert in Buckinghamshire).

Otherwise almost all medieval houses were TIMBER-FRAMED. This was true across most of England but the greatest numbers to have survived are in the south-east, East Anglia and the Midland counties. Precise dating of such buildings is often difficult, unless evidence from dendrochronology (the technique of dating timbers by analysis of their growth rings) is available. Because surviving timber-framed houses have served generations of inhabitants they have also frequently been much altered, and sometimes recased in brick or other materials, so that their original form may be far from obvious from the outside. Indeed, the only way to determine the medieval origin of some houses is to be prepared to crawl around in the roof space.

The principal type of hall house in the period up to the C14 was the AISLED HALL, which has much in common with the design of churches from the mid C12. Just as in churches, Anglo-Norman builders of domestic halls had to find a way of roofing a large space which would not restrict the width of the hall to the length of whatever timbers they could find to act as tie-beams and rafters. In order to overcome this they erected arcade posts, either of stone or timber, supporting the main roof beams, together with beams over the aisles flanking the central 'nave' of the hall. The most important example of an aisled hall is usually thought to be Westminster Hall, built by William II in 1097–9, but there is now some uncertainty about whether this had an aisled form before it was altered in the C14. At Oakham Castle, Rutland, the aisled hall built *c.* 1180–90 survives because it continued to serve as a court room for the town. Externally this hall strongly resembles an aisled church with a pitched roof over the taller nave and roofs of the lean-to type over the aisles. Aisled construction was also much used for medieval barns, where large floor areas were needed.

Although the aisled hall was the only solution for the large halls of great houses – including bishops' palaces, or the Great Hall at Winchester Castle, built by Henry III in the early C13 with quatrefoil piers of the Early English kind – it did not preclude its use in more modest houses. These lesser examples also include SINGLE-

12. Oakham Castle, Rutland, interior of the hall, built c. 1180–90. This is one of the best-preserved AISLED HALLS in England and can be dated by the style of its architecture and sculptural decoration to the last quarter of the C12. The interior might easily be mistaken for a Norman church, with its plain arcade piers of circular section. The capitals and arches of the arcade piers are carved with typical forms of Norman ornament from the late C12 Transitional phase, in which early Norman and Gothic forms are combined. These include enriched leafy CROCKETS and bands of DOGTOOTH, NAILHEAD and CHEVRON, the zigzag motif so prevalent in Norman buildings. At one end of the room were doors to the buttery and pantry. The entrance was in the side wall

▲ 13. Cressing Temple, Essex, barley barn, c. 1205–35. Although a large agricultural building, the timber structure of the barn shows how the interior of a medieval aisled hall might have appeared

AISLED HALLS, with the aisle running along one side of the house only. A greater number of such aisled halls survive from the C14 onwards, and more continue to come to light, but it is rare to find them unaltered.

Aisled halls can be found in smaller houses up to the C15, but from the C14 they began to fall out of favour among grander houses, where the presence of arcade piers in the space of the hall was regarded as intrusive. Innovations in roof construction (*see* p. 31), which used curved braces to spread the weight of the roof to the walls, provided the opportunity to remove them. A basic form of this is known as raised aisle construction, in which the arcade posts are placed above a tie beam that is set below the head of the wall.

From about the mid C13, many open hall houses employed CRUCK construction as an alternative to, or in combination with, aisled construction. This uses long curved timbers, known as blades, which are made by splitting the trunk and main branch of a single tree. They are tied together by other timbers to form the basic

▲ 14. Church Road, Weobley, Herefordshire. An example of full cruck construction in a hall house of probably C14 date. The blades of the cruck and
the collar tying them together are clearly displayed. This building began as
the two-bay hall of a four-bay house, so the truss exposed in the end wall
was originally internal

triangular or A-shaped truss of the frame that left the floorspace of
a hall unencumbered. The blades provide only the supporting structure for the roof, so the walls of a cruck house can be made from
timber infilled with other materials, such as stone, earth or turf. As
the walling is independent of the frame it is quite common to find
that walls have changed over time so that earth walls might have
been replaced later in stone or brick.

Cruck framing in houses is concentrated almost exclusively in the
western half of England, from north to south, and in Wales. It is possible that cruck frames were once more widespread in eastern areas
but that they have been superseded by other forms of construction;
in rural areas, where renewal in the C18 and C19 was less widespread
more have survived. Crucks are not necessarily a reliable guide to
dating houses, as this style of construction continued through and
beyond the Middle Ages (the few examples of cruck-frame houses
in the West Riding of Yorkshire, for example, are mostly C16, much
later than elsewhere). In English houses crucks were abandoned
among high status houses first, in the mid C15, but continued in use

▼ 15. The illustrations below show types of cruck frame. In a FULL CRUCK the blades stand on the floor and encompass the entire space of the room up to the ridge of the roof. A RAISED CRUCK is similar, but the blades start from the wall above floor level. A BASE CRUCK finishes at the collar so is not a true cruck. A JOINTED CRUCK has blades made from two pieces, the lower one forming the wall post, with a secondary blade jointed into it and forming the principal timber of the roof. In an UPPER CRUCK the blades are set on the wall-head and form only the roof structure, which gave greater headroom in houses with an upper storey or attic

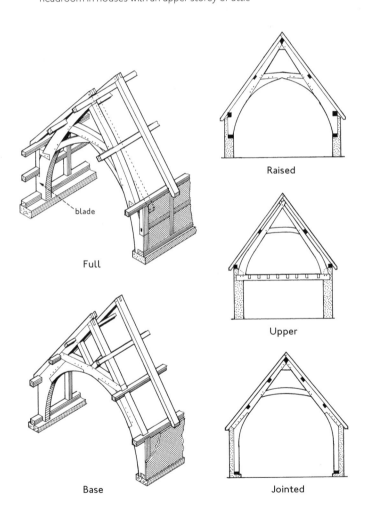

blade

Full

Base

Raised

Upper

Jointed

at the vernacular level for some time. Different areas favoured different forms of cruck construction: so for example in Devon, Somerset and Dorset and South Wales the preference for JOINTED CRUCKS lasts several centuries, yet in Cornwall this type is almost unheard of and the related form known as BASE CRUCKS are favoured instead. This is probably explained by the absence in parts of the country of timber suitable for creating long blades.

The second form of timber-framed construction widely used in the medieval period and after is BOX FRAMING, made up of wall-posts, wall-plates and tie-beams. This type of framing occurs alongside the cruck tradition but in many areas supplanted it as the dominant mode of construction until the timber-framing tradition died out in the C17. Box framing was superior to cruck framing for various reasons, perhaps most notably the fact that it made it possible to build higher than a single storey.

Up to the mid C15 the usual type of box framing is called large framing; it is usually braced for strength at its angles by shorter

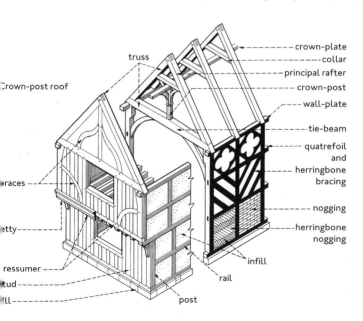

16. The components of BOX FRAMING including close studding and panel framing

▲ 17. Abbots House, Butcher Row, Shrewsbury, Shropshire. This row of shops with tenements was built in 1457–9 and demonstrates the increasing height of buildings on urban plots by the mid-C15 and the opportunity for display on a corner site. The building has two jetties running along the front and side and carved decoration to much of the timber structure. Note the combination of close-studding at first floor and square panels above

timbers, either arched or straight. square (or small) framing is a new form of the C15 and after, and is used across a large area of England from West Sussex in the South-East to Lancashire in the North-West. By contrast CLOSE-STUDDING is the popular form in the South-East and East Anglia after *c.* 1450. The principal upright timbers and the principal roof timbers divide the structure into regular units called bays, and determine the placing of windows and doors.

Many timber-framed houses have jetties, a device introduced already in some houses in the late C13 and prevalent in the C15–C17 by which the timbers of an upper floor project beyond the line of the floor below. The practice could be employed for three- or even four-storey buildings, with each storey stepping forward from the one below. Jetties might only be used at the front of the building, or to more than one side, or be reserved for the gables of the cross-wings. They were even used inside some medieval houses to increase the floor space of upper rooms in cross-wings by allowing them to project into the space of the hall. Jetties and the exposed frame in general also provided scope for conspicuous carved ornament; indeed the decision to jetty might be as much about display and status as any concern with increasing room sizes. It is quite usual to find that the ground floor of a house has later been reconstructed in brick or stone and the wall brought out to the line of the jetty, a technique known as underbuilding, which may disguise the fact that a house was originally jettied.

The beginning of the end of the timber-framed tradition came in the C15, when the use of brick was gradually introduced. There is scanty evidence for the use of brick in medieval houses, but what there is concentrated in the east of the country, where there is the remarkable early example of Little Wenham Hall, Suffolk, built in the late C13, which makes much use of locally made brick in concert

18. Paycocke's, Coggeshall, Essex. An exceptional, albeit restored, example of the fashion for close-studding in box-framed houses. This was built c. 1509 for a merchant and the gratuitous use of timbers closely spaced has as much to do with display of wealth as any structural concern. The infilling with diagonal patterns of brick is known as NOGGING

◄ 19. Layer Marney Tower, Essex, built c. 1520–5. One of the best examples of moulded Tudor brickwork with terracotta decoration for the windows and parapet

with other materials. It is then not used again for houses until the C15: examples include Falkbourne Hall, Essex (c. 1439); Tattershall Castle, Lincolnshire (begun 1434–5); Herstmonceux Castle, East Sussex (licence to crenellate given in 1441), and Someries Castle, Bedfordshire (begun c. 1445–7). By the late C15 brick was employed in major residences such as the Bishop of Lincoln's palace at Buckden, Huntingdonshire; and it was adopted as the material of choice for the most prestigious houses of the early Tudor period. Early and Tudor bricks are thinner and longer than bricks in later houses. Brick walls must be bonded for strength and stability and bricklayers developed a variety of methods of bonding resulting in different patterns of stretchers (sides) and headers (ends) in the walls of houses. A distinctive early form of bond, used in C15 and C16 houses, is ENGLISH BOND, renowned for its strength, in which the headers and stretchers are laid in alternate courses. This remained the dominant style of bonding in English brick building until the early C17. While this pattern of bonding is in itself decorative, the Tudor builders used blackened or burnt headers to create the familiar criss-cross patterns known as DIAPERING. The other novelty of the early C16 is use of moulded bricks for decoration, especially for chimneys (for which see p. 38–9) and TERRACOTTA decoration, which was moulded in finer clay and fired to achieve more sophisticated ornament.

Medieval roofs

What we know of roofs in houses before about the mid C13 is limited. stone vaults of the kind found in medieval churches are rare in domestic buildings except as the undercrofts of houses with first-floor halls or chamber blocks. Cruck buildings provided the roof structure as an integral part of the frame. In stone or box-framed buildings the roof was independent of the walls and the design of roofs in houses follows a similar pattern to those of medieval churches. The most common forms of roof are double-pitched (or gabled), with the walls of the ends of the house carried up to the point of the roof; HIPPED, with a triangular slope from the wall-head to the roof ridge; and HALF-HIPPED, with the end wall carried above the eaves but with its upper point squared off by a small hip. Another variant is the GABLETED roof, essentially identical to the hipped form but with the roof ridge raised slightly higher on two triangular sections at each end.

These different styles require roof frames of varied complexity. A most basic version is the SINGLE-FRAMED ROOF, with pairs of COMMON RAFTERS attached to the WALL-PLATE and pegged together to form a triangular roof shape. Such roofs were constructed without a timber forming the ridge of the roof, and are tied together near the apex of the roof by a COLLAR beam; the rafters and collar could be ceiled over to form a barrel vault.

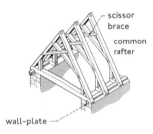

Scissor truss roof (single-framed)

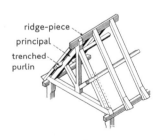

Kingpost roof (double-framed)

In stone houses the end gables of the walls provided reinforcement against the roof collapsing lengthways, but in timber-framed houses with roofs of hipped or half-hipped form other timbers were needed to join the rafters to reinforce them, unless larger TRUSSES spanning the roof were used to bear the load of the rafters. Medieval carpenters developed the DOUBLE-FRAMED ROOF which introduced PURLINS – extra horizontal timbers that run along the roof supporting the common rafters and send the weight from the rafters to the principal trusses. These were standard in cruck-framed buildings where the purlins attach to the backs of the cruck blades. In box-framed houses carpenters also introduced PRINCIPAL RAFT-ERS, larger than the common rafters and set at regular intervals, usually corresponding with the principal uprights of the wall frame. Where the purlins are set into these rafters the technique is known as a TRENCHED PURLIN roof. Where it is held between the collar and the rafter it is known as a CLASPED PURLIN roof. Later variants, associated with the later medieval period and beyond, are the BUTT PURLIN, where the purlins are attached (tenoned) into the rafters, and the THROUGH PURLIN, where the purlin passes through the rafter.

The standard roof type in houses in many areas from the C13 onwards was the KINGPOST ROOF. This has a tie-beam spanning between principal rafters, with a vertical post in the centre reaching to the ridge piece at the roof's apex. Braces could be introduced between the post and rafters for greater stability. The CROWN-POST roof (very popular in south-east England) is similar, but the central post supports a longitudinal member called a COLLAR-PURLIN (or CROWN PLATE) which carries the collars between the rafters. This support is further reinforced by short diagonal braces from the post to the collar (hence the 'crown'). At their most elaborate, crown-post roofs may have as many as four braces supporting the collar-purlin and the collars, and the central post may be carved to enhance visual interest in the roof over a hall. Another variant, more common from the late medieval period and after is the QUEEN-POST ROOF, in which there are two or more posts (or struts) evenly spaced on the tie-beam and supporting the purlins. The ARCH-BRACED ROOF – especially popular in the West Country – supported the principal rafters by means of curved timbers supported on WALL-POSTS and forming an arch, obviating the need for a tie-beam. The addition of decoration to the principal timbers was a sign of status and, as the early C16 hall at Cotehele shows, the addition of WIND-BRACES – curved

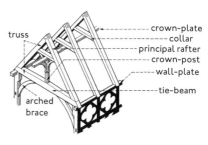

Crown-post roof

20. The Great Hall at Cotehele, Cornwall. Built c. 1520, it is an excellent example of an arch-braced roof with wind braces. By adding cusping to the braces impressive patterns are achieved

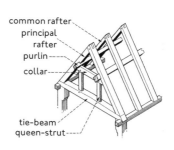

Queen-post roof (double-framed)

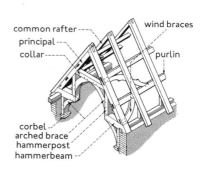

Hammerbeam roof

timbers laid against the inner side of the roof in the spaces between the purlins and rafters, and designed to strengthen the roof laterally against wind pressure – could be exploited to great decorative effect. Carvers also often lavished attention on the hall truss – the central roof truss over a hall two or more bays long, which is left open (unlike the trusses of the end walls which are infilled and thus closed), and can be clearly seen from below. This might be carved with decoration along the edge of the tie-beam, or given a carved BOSS at the apex of the arch in an arch-braced roof. Such carved open trusses are also sometimes found in the larger first-floor chambers of the solar cross-wing.

The grandest type of late medieval roof, used as much in churches as in houses, is the HAMMERBEAM ROOF, in which the upper roof timbers are cantilevered from a beam that projects from the wall and is supported by arched braces, thus overcoming the need to use aisle posts in order to span wide spaces. An early example of this is the roof of the Pilgrims' Hall in Winchester, dated to c. 1310–11 by dendrochronology. Hammerbeams were often decorated: elaborately carved hammerbeam roofs, sometimes in two tiers, became features of some C16 houses, such as Hampton Court Palace and the Great Hall at Burghley House.

Roof coverings varied, usually depending on the most appropriate available materials, so in many areas of east, south and southwest England thatching of reed or wheat is common; elsewhere turf was normally used. In stone areas, such as the Cotswolds or the Pennines, where the walls could carry the weight imposed, the roof might have stone flags. In the clay regions, flat, overlapping tiles or curved PANTILES are standard. Roof coverings change over time, so a medieval house which now has a tile roof may have been thatched originally. Both thatch and tile coverings needed steeply pitched roofs, while a shallow pitch is best for stone flags.

Medieval doors and windows

Domestic doors take a variety of shapes over the medieval period, similar to church doors. The principal shapes, whether of stone or timber, are TWO-CENTRED ARCHES (beginning early but in use for a long period); OGEE ARCHES (C14); SHOULDERED ARCHES (also known as 'Caernarvon' arches, late C13 onwards) and THREE-CENTRED and FOUR-CENTRED ARCHES (late C14 to C16). Stone doorways, like stone walls, are a feature of the highest status houses. C15 and C16 doorframes are often carved in the spandrels – the space between the arches and the enclosing rectangle around them - with foliage or heraldic emblems.

With the evolution of the more complex H-shaped plans of the C15 and the flooring over of open halls, many

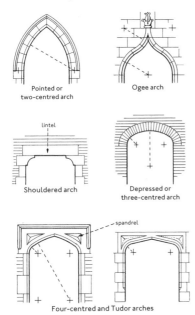

Pointed or two-centred arch

Ogee arch

lintel

Shouldered arch

Depressed or three-centred arch

spandrel

Four-centred and Tudor arches

Types of arches

21. Ockwells Manor House, Berkshire. Built *c.* 1450, its front is characteristic of the grander houses of the mid-C15 with two-storey crosswings, and a two-storey porch at the low end of the hall and opening into the cross passage. The windows at high level above plain walling indicate that the central hall is open to the roof. The bay to the r. with a small gable above two tiers of windows shows that this lights the high end of the hall. The larger canted bay to the r. has a solid band between the lower and upper windows indicating a two-storey interior for the solar

houses of higher status adopted two-storey porches as a protection for the door and also to provide an additional room at first-floor level. The usual placing of the entrance to medieval houses at the low end of the hall means that the porch is often tucked against the cross-wing at this end, but as the open hall disappeared and the internal plan of houses began to change, the entrance moves increasingly towards the centre of the front.

The placing of windows in medieval houses is a useful clue to the function and status of the rooms within, with the largest opening reserved for lighting the table at the high end of the hall. However, windows may have been replaced more than once in the lifetime of a house of early date, and the original position may no longer be obvious. The position of blocked openings can often be discerned

▲   22. Aydon Castle, Northumberland, solar window, c. 1280

in the frame of timber-framed buildings, and where later coverings of brick or plaster have been removed original windows may have survived or have been restored.

Medieval stone windows are found only in royal and ecclesiastical palaces. The styles of such windows vary, but show common design features with those of churches. The windows in the Jew's House, Lincoln (p. 19) had the familiar arched shape of Norman windows, with two lights separated by a mullion under a tympanum and a deep splay inside to increase the spread of light within. Some later house had stone LANCETS, and at the most prestigious levels windows might have various forms of BAR TRACERY, such as Y-TRACERY, enhanced by CUSPING on the arches of the windows, GEOMETRICAL TRACERY (mid to late C13), CURVILINEAR

TRACERY with double-curved OGEE mouldings (C14 and C15) and RETICULATED TRACERY (after c. 1330).

While tracery windows are predominantly stone windows, the same effects could be achieved on a small scale in timber. Tracery favoured upright openings and might be used only for the largest window in a hall house, lighting the high end of the hall or the great chamber. Windows in this positions were usually taller than the other windows and C15 and C16 examples, again following the developments in Perpendicular Gothic tracery, might even have a central horizontal rail (transom) dividing the lights into two tiers and a HOODMOULDING (the projecting moulding above an arch or lintel to throw off water). More commonly, C15 and C16 windows have a straight-headed form with a horizontal hoodmould often known as a LABEL MOULDING, with SPLAYED MULLIONS (stone) or

▼ 23. Manor House, Northborough, Peterborough, c. 1320–40.
   Reticulated tracery in a domestic context

DIAMOND MULLIONS (timber). These could range from two-lights to long sequences of multiple lights (e.g. at Ockwells, p. 37). Mullioned windows continued in use in smaller houses and cottages much later than in large houses, where this form disappeared at the end of the C17. In the early period there was no glazing in windows of most houses. Instead, draughts and light were kept out by shutters. Only later and only in the most expensive houses was glazing created by inserting small quarries of glass into lead frames attached to the window mullions. For modest houses this change would not take place until after *c.* 1600.

The very largest medieval houses, and those of the late C15 and earlier C16, had three-sided BAY WINDOWS lighting the high end of the hall or other important rooms and filling much of the wall space between the ground and eaves of the roof (e.g. the tall bay window added to Fawsley Hall, Northants). When placed at the high end of the hall these are sometimes also known as ORIEL WINDOWS, although the same term usually applies to projecting first-floor windows supported on corbels, notably over the entrance or in the gatehouse. The same term is sometimes applied to the box-like windows on brackets in timber-framed buildings.

In late medieval timber buildings the opportunities for carved decoration are exploited. As C15 and C16 houses developed cross-wings with GABLED ends, decoration was also applied to BARGE-BOARDS fixed beneath the eaves of the gable to protect the rafters, *see* Ockwells p. 37. These are sometimes pierced or fretted with patterns, such as quatrefoils, or carved with popular motifs such as trailing leaf vine or castellation.

▶ 24. Fawsley Hall, Northamptonshire, hall oriel window, c. 1530. This is a lavish example of a tall projecting window lighting the high end of the hall. The lights are in three tiers and have transoms with castellation, like many church windows of the Perp phase. Typical of C15 and early C16 domestic windows the arches of the frame and the individual lights are four-centred and have hollow spandrels. At the base of the bay window are carved emblems of shields in quatrefoils, another very prevalent motif in C15 and early C16 architecture. The extra storey above the eaves of the roof is very unusual feature and its original purpose unknown

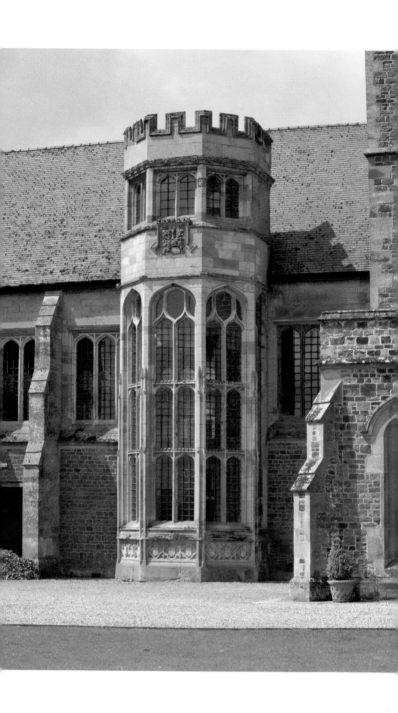

Details: interior fittings and decoration

The interior of the medieval house was just as important to its owners as ours are to us. Status might be expressed in the way the hall was divided from the cross-passage. This could take the form of a low SCREEN, or in grander houses a SPERE (a screen of full height) – popular over a long period in the north of England – when the roof truss marking the line of the screens passage becomes the top member of a fixed structure that divides the hall from the passage, with a wide central opening flanked by short walls. The opening would also have a fixed or moveable screen.

At the opposite end there was another timber partition between the hall and the solar, with PANELLING of plank-and-muntin type and a door to the parlour. This screen might have a bench fixed to the wall for the raised DAIS on which the high table was set, and occasionally this would be given further definition by a DAIS CANOPY fixed to the partition.

As houses expanded in the Tudor period some halls were divided into two storeys although this process usually took place in most houses much later. This created the dilemma of how to disperse smoke from the fire that was formerly lit in the central hearth. In early houses it simply escaped through a vent in the roof called a LOUVRE; surviving medieval roofs in houses may still have soot-blackened timbers to indicate that they were originally open over the hall. The SMOKE BAY was the earliest form of what we would recognize as a fireplace and chimney. A partition was formed in the roof trusses closing off the bay over the hearth and controlling the passage of smoke to the louvre. A variation on this and a precursor to later brick and stone chimneys was the SMOKE HOOD, suitable for floored or unfloored halls, which was a funnel constructed of timber against the 'low' end of the hall to direct smoke upwards to a narrow chimney piercing the roof.

▶ 25. Rufford Old Hall, Lancashire, c. 1530. An outstanding example of a SPERE, the screen separating the hall from the screens passage. In the centre of the full-height opening is an elaborately carved moveable partition. Behind, in the far wall of the passage doors lead to the kitchen, buttery, pantry and probably the stairs to the chamber over the service rooms

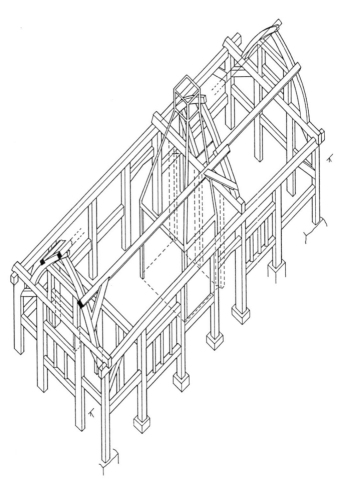

▲   26. Snug Hall, Birtles, Cheshire. This axonometric projection illustrates
    how a smoke hood might be built against the partition at the low end of
    an open hall and thereby also serve the hearth of the adjoining room

Fireplaces built into walls were already a feature of the private
rooms in the two-storey chamber blocks of the more important
medieval stone houses. Norman fireplaces, of which a few survive
in castles, are round-arched and sometimes ornamented with the
patterns found on Norman doors, arches and windows. C13 and C14
fireplaces are hooded, often of a pyramidal shape, and project from
the wall face (e.g. the Prior's House, Ely, Cambs.) on shafts or brackets. Fireplaces with FOUR-CENTRED ARCHES are the standard

type for the C15 and most of the C16 (and even later) in the shallower form of four-centred arch known as the TUDOR ARCH. The more elaborate examples might incorporate a decorative frieze of patterns following contemporary fashion (e.g. quatrefoils in circles, heraldic devices or blind tracery and a cresting), and among the later types the spandrels are carved with foliage, just as in the arches of Tudor doorcases and gateways. The presence of several heated rooms in a house could be ostentatiously indicated by its CHIMNEYSTACKS, and a virtue was made of the design of their stacks: in the early to mid C16 these take a variety of forms including twisted and diamond patterns. Such chimneystacks became *de rigueur* in noble houses and a key emblem of status.

As floors were inserted into the height of the hall, the decoration of roof trusses – now concealed from view – became unimportant. Instead, most attention was given to the beams and JOISTS supporting the floors. In some instances, by the earlier C16 boarded

▲ 28. Longthorpe Tower, Longthorpe, Peterborough, wall paintings executed c. 1310–29, one of the few examples in England of C14 domestic wall painting, with allegorical and biblical scenes as well as decorative patterns painted all over the wall surfaces and vaulted ceiling of the first-floor room

▲ 29. Carlisle Cathedral, Cumbria. Deanery, ceiling. Schemes of painted decoration often include decoration of other motifs that give a clue as to their date. This example has mottoes and badges of Prior Senhouse, who was prior of Carlisle from 1500–20. Black, red and white are the most widely used colours in medieval and C16 wallpainting. The most expensive pigment was green

ceilings were introduced and used to carry decoration in the form of patterns of ribs. Alternatively the panels of the ceiling would be plastered. On the walls, the more important houses from the C13 onwards had WAINSCOTTING (panelling). This would have been the simplest plank-and-muntin type, until the introduction of LINENFOLD PANELLING in the superior houses of the late C15 and early C16.

Much of this panelling would have been painted originally: painted decoration of walls and ceilings was far more widespread

30. Parlour, Haddon Hall, Derbyshire. The beam of the ceiling has been CHAMFERED and moulded and stopped where it meets the wall. In rooms where later partitions have been introduced, the position of stops will often give the best clue to the original layout. The PANELLING with coats of arms is dated 1545

in the medieval period and up to the mid C16 than one might think. Although paintings are recorded in many of the most important houses, survivals of any kind are extremely rare. Most of the surviving paintwork in houses, however, is no earlier than the first half of the C16 (for which *see* below) and again the preserve of the wealthiest houses. In the next century painted interiors extended to the yeoman and merchant class.

2 ELIZABETHAN AND JACOBEAN HOUSES, c. 1550–1625

The Dissolution of the Monasteries in the 1530s had presented many courtiers with opportunities for remodelling the buildings of former monastic establishments. Much good building material that could be carted away for construction and reconstruction also became available. Increasing wealth from the wool and cloth trades in parts of England created fortunes at various levels of society that were invested in new buildings, and during this period the gentry class of knights and squires, who derived income from their landholdings, expanded greatly. Concern for defence diminished and emphasis on display increased. At the same time the redistribution of wealth which followed the changes in land ownership was spread further down the social scale and the Elizabethan and Jacobean years of the late C16 and early C17 became a boom period for the building of manor houses, farmhouses and cottages – a process sometimes referred to as the 'Great Rebuilding'.

▲ 31. Titchfield Abbey, Hampshire. Sir Thomas Wriothesley's Caen stone gate-house of 1538, driven through the nave of the former monastic church

The notion of a 'Great Rebuilding' in English houses was first identified by W. G. Hoskins in 1953. He proposed that during the late C16 and early C17 the vast proportion of medieval housing in the countryside was replaced, as the minor gentry and better-off farmers embarked on a concerted period of new building, adopting many of the features of the houses of their social superiors. In the period since the publication of Hoskins's theory historians have contested how, when and where this took place and have shown that at the very least the process occurred at different times in the various regions of England, depending among other factors on the economic circumstances of those areas. The ability to date timbers has also conclusively proved the survival of many medieval houses of the 'peasant' class which earlier historians assumed to have been too poorly built to survive. In the southern and eastern counties the rebuilding seems to come earliest, but in the Pennine areas of the West Riding of Yorkshire, for example, it occurs only in the early to mid C17, where new houses of stone were built by the gentry. It is indisputable, however, that this period saw considerable transformation of existing houses by their owners.

32. Tudor House, Godmanchester, Huntingdonshire, built 1600–03. This house was erected for a wealthy farmer and the dates of its construction are carved on the façade. Dates inscribed on houses are much more common from the late C16 onwards

Plan and structure

The ELIZABETHAN period (1558–1603) produced some remarkable houses. Prosperity paid for greater comfort in warmer, better-lit houses with improved sanitation. In many ways, the houses of this period were little different from those of the late medieval and earlier Tudor period in how they were organized, with a clear division between the high and low ends of the house and the placing of the best rooms on the upper floor.

The most striking innovation in Elizabethan houses that distinguishes them from the period before *c.* 1550 is the desire for symmetry and height in elevation, combined with a concentration of the floor plan into a more compact form. This is the period in which a unity of architectural form and style starts to take precedence over the medieval tradition of expressing the hierarchy of the different elements of the house (high end–hall–low end) through the emphasis given to each part. Elizabethan house-builders wished their homes to clearly express their position in society and their taste and learning – especially their understanding of the principles of Classicism, which had spread to England from Renaissance Europe.

These innovations are first seen in the great houses but filtered down the social scale through the C16 and C17. Queen Elizabeth herself was an architectural patron of marginal importance and the innovators were instead her senior courtiers, many of whom were new men rather than the offspring of noble families with existing seats. Others rode high on the expansion of the legal profession or the opportunities for enrichment in the commercial world, particularly in the wool and textile trade.

Kirby Hall, Northamptonshire, begun in 1570, is a courtyard house of traditional late medieval plan with an outer and inner court. But it is distinguished from earlier houses by the symmetrical treatment of the hall elevation in the inner court and the use of classical orders. At Kirby, and other earlier houses of its type, the important elevations are those around the courtyard. The external elevations are much less important and often of incoherent appearance with chimneys, garderobes and other protrusions. So houses of this kind are described as inward-looking. The second trans-

33. Kirby Hall, Northamptonshire, courtyard, N front 1560, remodelled c. 1630. Houses of the late medieval and Tudor period expressed the hierarchy of the hall and the adjoining rooms at the high and low ends in an asymmetric elevation, with the porch off-centre and large windows denoting the hall on one side. The internal arrangements of the hall range at Kirby are no different, but here the designers have imposed a symmetrical façade, with the porch in the centre. By applying a giant order of pilasters to the façades of both the (open) hall on its right and the two-storey range on its left, and by making the windows match (while blocking the middle band of lights to allow for the floor within the two-storey range), seamless uniformity is achieved

formation in the Elizabethan house is the design of houses to have an outward-looking form, in which the external elevations are the most important. The most significant of these is Longleat, Wiltshire, reconstructed from 1572 and completed c. 1580, where there is absolute symmetry of all four façades; unsightly chimneys and staircase towers are placed on the inner façades. Gradually the courtyard plan was abandoned in the great houses.

△ 34. Shaw House, Newbury, Berkshire. An H-plan house built 1579–82 with a perfectly symmetrical front in which every element – wings, gables and even the window designs – is an exact mirror of the other half (the windows on the right on the ground floor were lengthened in the C18)

The transition to an outward-facing design and progress towards a more compact plan and symmetrical elevation can also be seen in in the burgeoning number of GENTRY HOUSES of the late C16 and early C17. Many of these begin to adopt a standard H-plan or E-plan front, with the middle stem formed by the porch (e.g. Montacute, Somerset). Their symmetry of elevation makes it increasingly difficult to 'read' the function of the various parts of the house.

At the same time other houses adopted an altogether more compressed form. There are numerous examples across England by the late C16 and early C17 of houses with compact, almost square appearance and symmetrical façades.

Under the influence of this desire for symmetry in elevation, the internal planning of Elizabethan and Jacobean houses also evolved. At Hardwick (New) Hall in Derbyshire (1590–9), the hall is turned through ninety degrees so that it runs through the very centre of the house from front to back. The entrance is therefore in the centre of the front elevation and at one end of the hall. Although Hardwick is an exceptionally grand house this innovation is notable because the hall is now somewhat reduced to the function of a passage, albeit a very generous one, for visitors on their way to the grand staircase,

35. Montacute House, Somerset. An example of an E-plan house, built c. 1595–1601, that illustrates the change to a fully symmetrical house front where it is no longer possible to make assumptions about the position, hierarchy and functions of the rooms within

36. Plan of Hardwick Hall, Derbyshire, 1590–9

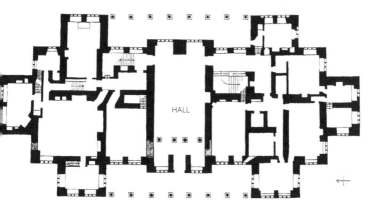

HALL

which was set off the far end of the hall and ascended to the most important rooms on the upper floor.

Although the innovation of the plan of Hardwick was not taken up immediately elsewhere, the continued decline of the hall as the principal room of the house is notable in houses of varied size through the late C16 and early C17. As has already been noted, in the largest houses it had ceased to be the room in which the family ate even before the C16. That function had been adopted by the best room in the private solar wing. In smaller houses the hall was floored over and in both cases its status was reduced to that of an outer reception room. In late C16 houses, the hall was single-storey from the beginning. This does not imply, however, that the hall lost its distinction, especially in the largest houses where it remained the centre of welcome and hospitality to visitors. In the largest houses of the C16 and C17, however, increased importance was afforded to the great chamber, which lay either on the first floor of the cross-wing or, in a fully floored house, immediately above the single-storey hall. This was the room in which the family not only ate but also lived and entertained, and there was usually a separate PARLOUR sharing some of the same functions. In medium-sized and smaller houses the number, size and purpose of these rooms would be scaled accordingly.

The great chamber was just one room incorporated into the evolving plan of larger C16 and C17 great houses that now contained suites of apartments for the lord and lady, including a withdrawing chamber and best bedchamber beyond the great chamber. A handful of the most select houses, like Theobalds, Lord Burghley's house just outside London, extended to royal lodgings – with at the very least a chamber for audiences, known as the 'presence chamber', a 'privy chamber' for eating, and a bedchamber with closet – in anticipation of having to accommodate the monarch and entourage, who embarked annually on a 'progress' from London to the various parts of the kingdom. The planning of these rooms followed the precedent of the royal palaces, and the greatest Jacobean houses (Hatfield, Herts.; Audley End, Essex; Bramshill, Hants.) could provide one suite for the king and another for the queen. Others of lesser means who were selected for a royal visit would have to adapt their own rooms to the monarch's requirements.

In the sequence of rooms that moved from the public space of the great chamber to the most private and smallest room (known as the closet), the climax was often a long gallery, designed among other activities for exercise. Galleries were already a feature of some courtiers' houses in the early C16 – the Long Gallery at The Vyne, Hampshire (1520s), is one of the earliest examples to be found

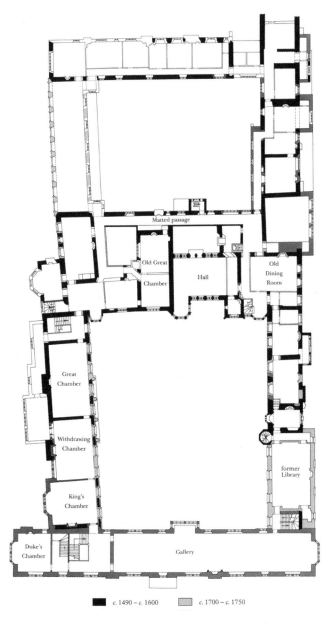

Matted passage

Old Great
Chamber

Hall

Old
Dining
Room

Great
Chamber

Withdrawing
Chamber

King's
Chamber

former
Library

Duke's
Chamber

Gallery

■ *c.* 1490 – *c.* 1600   □ *c.* 1700 – *c.* 1750

▲   37. Apethorpe Hall, plan of first floor

39. Little Moreton Hall, Cheshire, s range, 1560s and late c16. The continuous band of windows on the top floor indicate the position of the long gallery

38. The Vyne, Hampshire. The door from the Long Gallery created in the 1520s. The carved overdoor and the emblems in the linenfold panelling make clear that this would have opened into the private suite of royal apartments

outside a royal household – but it is primarily a product of the late c16 and early c17. The greatest of these galleries are more than 100 ft (30 metres) long. Such galleries also provided opportunities to overlook the gardens surrounding the house, while some have recesses akin to small rooms into which guests could retreat for more private activity. Although long galleries were *de rigueur* for suites of apartments in great houses, they appear also in lesser gentry houses of this period, either placed next to the great chamber on the first floor or sometimes at the very top of the house, as at Little Moreton Hall, Cheshire, where the long gallery is placed on the top floor of the south wing.

The changes and improvements in these larger houses are paralleled in medium and smaller houses of the vernacular kind. By the mid-C16 such houses were becoming fully floored, so that the central range of a typical three-unit house was now two-storey, comprising a hall below a chamber. This process of horizontal subdivision extended down to ordinary cottages by the end of the C17. Many houses also adopted an ATTIC FLOOR for storage, the accommodation of servants or both. New houses of medium size in the C17 were designed with the expectation of a useable attic floor, often indicated by a staircase that rises the full height of the house.

Houses in the towns in the late C16 and early C17 adopt a different form from their medieval predecessors. As in other types of house the open hall which had been a central feature of the medieval town house disappeared in the C16 in favour of a best chamber on the first floor and larger numbers of rooms on the upper floors. Houses thus became shallower and increasingly tall with three, four, or even five storeys, often with jetties at each level, e.g. Staple Inn, Holborn, London.

Accompanying this trend was the more widespread introduction of CHIMNEYS. These could be placed laterally – on the long side wall – or axially, at one end of the hall. In new houses the chimney would be designed as an integral part of the plan – in stone houses usually in the end gables or laterally placed – but older houses could also be adapted to incorporate one. Through the C16, one standard plan that results from this change is the hearth-passage plan, in which the entrance cross-passage ran though the depth of the house behind the chimney in the hall (whether still open to the roof or not).

The LOBBY ENTRY plan appears in the late C16, primarily in timber houses, when chimneys were built into the old cross passage, blocking it and leaving just a lobby inside the door with the hall to one side and the service rooms to the other. An obvious advantage is that a chimney in this position could heat two rooms. In larger houses the arrangement of rooms was sometimes reversed so that the parlour could be placed beside the entrance, with a fireplace sharing the chimney in the old passage, and the kitchen moved to the other end of the house with its own entrance. If the traditional

40. Bramley Manor, Bramley, Hampshire, c. 1545–6, is an example of a house with a hearth-passage plan. This is indicated by the position of the door in relation to the chimney. The parlour in the wing to the left has its own chimneystack built against the side wall. This type of plan went out of fashion in Hampshire just a few years after this house was built, but it remained quite common until much later elsewhere

arrangement was kept, a separate chimney might be added on the gable end for the parlour.

Needless to say there are numerous variations on this basic plan. The simplest is called a BAFFLE ENTRY, where the door opens directly into the rooms to left and right without a lobby. On the opposite side of the chimney from the door there was now a convenient space for a spiral staircase: in such houses, if the actual stair no longer survives, there is often a clear indication in the framing that this was its former position.

Details: exterior

The influence of the RENAISSANCE came gradually to English houses. To begin with the effects may be seen in the adoption of stylistic motifs in the decoration or ornament of houses and their interiors, co-existing with the continuation of medieval styles. A small coterie of courtiers in the mid-c16, notably those associated with Edward Seymour 1st Duke of Somerset, who acted as Lord Protector to Edward VI after the death of Henry VIII in 1547 had approached the Renaissance as a style rather than mere decoration. Somerset's own house in the Strand in London is credited with an early use of the classical orders (*see* p. 74) in the correct manner. Familiarity with the principles of classicism became an emblem of learning, demonstrated by the incorporation of the orders in the great houses associated with the Elizabethan and Jacobean courtiers, such as Burghley, Kirby Hall and Longleat.

Also very characteristic of the large houses of this period is a BALUSTRADE or pierced parapet wall further emphasising the height of the three-storey elevations now being achieved in houses such as Hardwick. In a few remarkable instances the parapet is composed of text, such as the inscription added to Temple Newsam House, near Leeds, in 1628, swearing allegiance to the king.

Another very obvious feature of Elizabethan and Jacobean houses is the addition of BAY WINDOWS to the elevation of two or more storeys. These feature in most of the largest houses of the Elizabethan phase. Some are square, others are canted, while others take a complex form of semicircular bows flanked by quarter-circles.

▶ 41. Burghley House, Peterborough, inner courtyard, built c. 1576–85 for Sir William Cecil, one the most powerful of Elizabeth's courtiers. The courtyard elevations exhibit many of typically Elizabethan motifs, including open parapets and balustrades, coats of arms, obelisk finials, patterns of circles in squares, niches with shell carving. THE FRONTISPIECE – an example of a 'tower of orders' – is dated 1585; the inscription of dates on buildings is far more common from this period onwards

▶ 42. New Hall, Boreham, Essex. An extravagant use of canted bay windows in the N range built by the 3rd Earl of Sussex after 1573

ELIZABETHAN AND JACOBEAN HOUSES, c. 1550–1625   61

▲ 43. Grimshaw Hall, Knowle, late C16

TIMBER-FRAMING becomes more elaborate in the C16 and C17, with curved braces and patterns of lozenges, saltires and quatrefoils filling the squares of the frame. This is used to outstanding decorative effect in parts of the Midlands, Cheshire (e.g. Little Moreton Hall, p. 57) and Lancashire well into the C17. Timber-framing remained dominant in several counties until the end of the C17, but in many areas the use of brick and stone spread increasingly to the level of the manor house and farmhouse.

In houses where a floor was inserted in the C16 or C17 this may be denoted by the introduction of DORMER WINDOWS to light the new upper chamber or the attic, as rooms at this level became more common. Houses built with a third storey from the outset favour multiple GABLES, not only on the wings but sometimes over each bay of the elevation and incorporating the attic windows. The classic type of Cotswold stone farmhouse with two or three gables dates from this period. The standard shape of gable in the late C16 is straight (i.e. triangular and steeply pitched), giving way to the SHAPED GABLE, with convex and concave curved sides. The

44. Toseland Hall, Huntingdonshire, built in 1608. By the early C17 some houses had started to adopt an almost square plan with regular gabled elevations unencumbered by chimneys

DUTCH or FLEMISH GABLE, which has a pediment at the head of the gable, is most prevalent in eastern England (Norfolk, Suffolk and Essex) and may well derive from contact with the Low Countries.

Windows in late C16 and early C17 houses are straight-headed; at Wollaton, Nottinghamshire, and Hardwick (New) Hall in Derbyshire, large grids of windows become *the* dominant feature of the elevation. By the early C17 MOULDINGS on window frames and window MULLIONS commonly change from flat chamfers to OVOLO (egg-shaped), OGEE (double-curved) or CAVETTO (concave or hollow chamfers) mouldings. Glass was produced in greater quantities in England during the C16 but it was still a luxury item and for the late C16 elite to build great houses with extensive areas of glazing was a conspicuous display of wealth. Windows of the period are composed of small pieces of glass to be set in lead frames ('cames'). C16 leading patterns for glass are typically diamond pattern, in the C17 typically rectangular.

Details: interior

Although the open hall disappeared from most houses in the C16, many of the largest houses retained one for reasons of prestige and status. To appreciate this one need only consider the considerable attention given to the design and decoration of SCREENS between halls and service passages into the Jacobean period. Similarly, the improvements made in the heating of rooms with fireplaces places new emphasis on their architectural character in late C16 and C17 houses as a vehicle for considerable ornament and decoration in wood, marble or stone.

As rooms on the upper floor of houses were given greater emphasis, the style and appearance of staircases became significant.

▲   45. Knole, Kent, Great Staircase, 1605/8

Straight flights of stairs from one level to another (e.g. from hall to great chamber in the adjoining wing) or spiral or winder stairs in turrets had been the norm in larger medieval and early C16 houses, and continued in many new houses until 1600; several Elizabethan houses, such as Melford Hall, Suffolk, make a display of such turrets in the angle between the main range and the wings of the house. In the great houses of the later C16 such as Burghley or Hardwick, great effort is made to create a sense of drama in the ascent to the principal rooms, and by the early C17 the principal staircase in a house grows increasingly spacious. In many relatively modest houses the staircase was something new in this period as chimneys made smoke-free upper floors more habitable. Typically it was accommodated against the chimneystack of the hall. The WELL STAIRCASE was becoming standard by this date. This type rises round the wall in three flights supported on one side by the wall and on the other by a CLOSED STRING, the beam running between the newel posts, into which the treads of each flight are jointed. Between the string and handrail is space for a BALUSTRADE. Both newels and balustrade offer themselves as opportunities for carved decoration and ornament. An extravagant example is the staircase at Knole, Kent (1605–10). The DOG-LEG STAIRCASE, with two flights running in opposite directions with a landing halfway, becomes the most common form of all from the early C17 onwards. Late C16 and early C17 staircases often have shaped PENDANTS from the bottom of newels on the upper flights and FINIALS to the newel at the base of the stair. BALUSTERS are usually turned, symmetrical for their length, and sometimes have incised lines for decoration. For later C17 baluster types *see* p. 95.

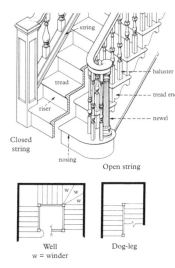

▲ 46. Long Gallery, Lanhydrock House, Cornwall, plasterwork, completed c. 1640

As floors were inserted into the space of the hall, so concealing the view up into the roof, the decoration of roof trusses became unimportant. Instead most attention was given to beams and JOISTS: in the richest areas of England at this period – notably East Anglia and the South-East – these were elaborately carved.

The fashion for plaster decoration, which could more cheaply produce the decorative effects of carved timber for ceilings and overmantels, was spread from the later C16 when it was first used in the town and country houses of aristocrats and courtiers and reached its peak in the first half of the C17 among lesser homes. At first, plaster ceilings imitate the style of timber ones and at their most elaborate have pendants, bosses and heraldic decoration, but patterns of STRAPWORK – flat bands forming geometric designs – were introduced in the late C16, much influenced by engravings

47. Red Lodge, Bristol, *c.* 1577–85; Great Oak Room, exhibiting the range of decorative detail in Elizabethan interiors

imported from the Netherlands (*see* p. 68), followed by enriched ribs, in which patterns of ornament were applied to the surface of the rib. A fine, if late, example is the ceiling of the Long Gallery at Lanhydrock, Cornwall, executed *c.* 1640. While much plasterwork is purely decorative in appearance, there was a strong enthusiasm in the early C17 for depictions of biblical or allegorical scenes in plasterwork, again often derived from prints, especially for overmantels. There is an especially strong tradition of this type of interior work in Somerset, Devon and Cornwall, although a very luxurious example is the fireplace and overmantel of the drawing room at Langleys, Great Waltham, Essex (*c.* 1620).

Wall coverings employ a variety of motifs in the C16 and early C17. SQUARE PANELLING, where grids of moulded vertical and horizontal rails frame a plain panel, is a common, basic C16 type.

▲ 48. Hill Hall, Theydon Mount, Essex, wall paintings of c. 1570

Under the influence of the Renaissance other motifs appear including portrait heads in medallions, masks and foliage decoration. The style of much joinery was, like plasterwork, greatly influenced by Netherlandish prints, and many of the same motifs occur in both. Towards the end of the C16 and continuing into the early C17 arcaded panelling appears (*see* Red Lodge, Brisol): an early Jacobean type is the geometric pattern of a square within a square or a diamond within a square.

At the most basic level the greater comfort achieved by glazing windows in houses was enhanced by plastering over of walls. painted decoration is much common from the mid-C16 forwards. Much was unsophisticated but the various types include texts, painted scenes and figures, especially imitation textile hangings and panelling. One of the most advanced sequence of paintings commissioned in this period, and a rare survival of figurative painting, is that at Hill Hall, Essex, the house of Sir Thomas Smith, built *c.* 1566–73. The staircase at Knole, Kent, is another good example of a scheme of decorative painted panels of strapwork and allegorical scenes, including the Four Ages of Man. Even if no pictorial decoration was attempted it was still a badge of status to paint interior woodwork in expensive green or red pigments.

▲ 52. Chevening House, Kent, as built in the 1620s. Detail of estate map, 1679

It was only in the C18 and C19, however, that the terrace would come to be the dominant type of house in cities and towns (*see* p. 87).

Chevening House in Kent, built in the 1620s by the 13th Lord Dacre, perhaps best represents the new image for domestic architecture promoted by Inigo Jones: gables are replaced with an overall HIPPED ROOF roof with a flat centre; the Elizabethan style of mullion and transom windows gives way to vertically proportioned casements; and the house is built to a rectangular DOUBLE-PILE PLAN (i.e. two rooms deep). Chevening has the simplest and most compact form of such a plan, containing a central hall and saloon with smaller rooms arranged around them. This plan shows on the elevations, which are entirely symmetrical.

It is not surprising that it took some time for the model of a severe classical villa to be assimilated into the existing tradition of country house building. The Civil War and Commonwealth periods (1642–60) were hardly propitious for a style associated with the court. However, the period of Cromwell's rule did produce one significant house closely following the Jonesian tradition and a handful of houses broadly acquainted with its principles.

THE ORDERS

The **orders** are the formalized versions of the post-and-lintel system in classical architecture. Engravings of the hierarchy of the five main orders appeared in the first volume of Sebastiano Serlio's *L'Architettura* (1537) but John Shute was the first English writer to publish the orders in his *First and Chief Groundes of Architecture* (1563).

The five main orders are: **Doric**, with its close cousin **Tuscan**; **Ionic**; **Corinthian**; and **composite**. You will also see a number of variants, often used in conjunction with these main types.

The **classical orders** differ from the columns of other styles and traditions in that they share certain codified forms. The columns have upwardly tapering shafts of fixed or limited proportions, distinctive **capitals** (the section at the top), and – usually – a distinctive **base**.

Each type is accompanied by its own treatment of the **entablature** – the term for the beam that spans between the columns. This is generally divided horizontally into three. The lowest division, usually left plain, is the **architrave**. In the middle is the **frieze**, which may be decorated or sculpted. The top section, which projects furthest, is the **cornice** (a term sometimes used loosely for the whole entablature). It too is often embellished, usually with abstract architectural forms. Strictly the distances between the columns are also regulated, to preserve harmony of proportion, although paired, grouped and even overlapping columns are not unusual. Columns used together in this way are called a **colonnade**.

Many buildings are unsuited to the use of free-standing columns. In these cases columns are sometimes **engaged**, that is they seem to be set into the wall. Sometimes half-columns appear, some-

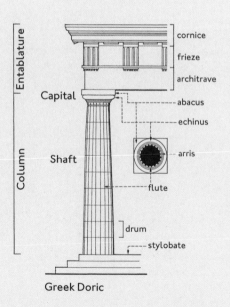

Greek Doric

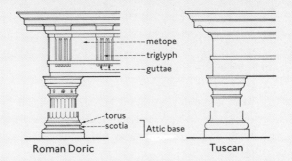

metope
triglyph
guttae

torus
scotia
] Attic base

Roman Doric

Tuscan

times three-quarter columns; quarter-columns are used for inner corners. The same range of treatments also appears in interiors.

Still more common is the use of the **pilaster**, a column represented in relief. Sometimes pilasters are made to overlap with each other, or with engaged columns.

Antae are a variant seen in Greek architecture, with straight sides and a very simple capital; free-standing columns set between antae or pilasters are said to be *in antis*.

Strictly speaking, every column should have its own entablature, but the reverse is not the case: many buildings have full classical entablatures but no columns or pilasters supporting them. These buildings without columns are known as **astylar**.

Most ordinary **Georgian** house fronts (see p. 107) belong in this category, though often the entablatures and openings are very plain, and the classical spirit of the whole is limited to the general proportions of the storeys.

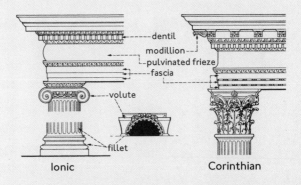

dentil
modillion
pulvinated frieze
fascia

volute

fillet

Ionic

Corinthian

Coleshill House in Berkshire by Sir Roger Pratt, completed *c.* 1658–62, though now demolished, is a perfect example of how the basic compact form of the double-pile plan of Chevening can be elongated to produce a more generous layout, in which the rectangular plan is divided in two on its long and short axes. Coleshill had six rooms, with the entrance hall and saloon (successor to the great chamber of the medieval house) in the centre. The hall also contained the staircase, ranged round two sides and arriving at a gallery on the first floor. This established the hall's new role as an entrance rather than the place for entertainment or dining; and at Coleshill Pratt acknowledged this by creating a servants' hall in the basement where they would dine – an important separation that heralded an end to medieval tradition. A cross axis is created by a passage running the full length of the house, leading to subsidiary backstairs – again keeping servants away from their masters – at either end.

A similarly sophisticated example of the same period is Thorpe Hall, Peterborough, which was built for Oliver St John, Lord Chief

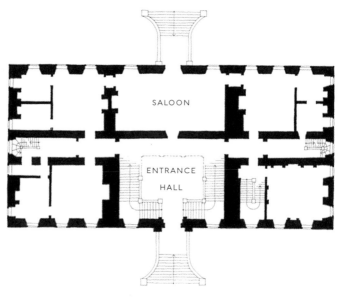

SALOON

ENTRANCE
HALL

▲　53. Coleshill House, Berkshire, plan

▲ 54. Thorpe Hall, Longthorpe, Peterborough by Peter Mills, begun 1654

Justice of the Common Pleas, during the Commonwealth. The house was designed by Peter Mills, a surveyor and twice master of the Tylers and Bricklayers Company in the City of London. Like Coleshill it is a façade of the ASTYLAR type (classical in their proportions but without actual orders in the form of pilasters). Thorpe Hall has a squarer plan than Coleshill and is in fact a triple pile (three rooms deep), but it is also a little old-fashioned in maintaining the tradition of a screens passage, with hall to one side, that runs right through the house as a corridor from the entrance to the garden door. As at Coleshill, the chimney flues are now taken into the inner walls of the house to avoid upsetting the symmetry of the façades and within each room are placed centrally to one wall, introducing to the interior the same experience of classical symmetry found without.

Houses of the Coleshill type have big HIPPED ROOFS and DORMER WINDOWS surmounted by PEDIMENTS – alternating triangular and segmental – a roof platform enclosed by a balustrade, high chimneystacks with far-projecting cornices, and a belvedere cupola. The windows at Thorpe Hall are of the early to mid-C17 classical house type: vertical and rectangular with a central mullion and a transom crossing two-thirds of the way up. For obvious reasons this is known as a CROSS-WINDOW. The other window type that is introduced for the first time in the early C17, notably at Wilton House, Wiltshire (begun in 1636), is the SERLIAN (or VENETIAN) WINDOW (*see* p. 100) which was published in Sebastiano Serlio's *Architettura* (1537–75) but ultimately derives from Palladio.

The austere Italian forms promoted by Inigo Jones and his followers were not widely influential beyond the limits of court circles. Many more houses of the earlier C17, while being progressive in terms of adopting the double-pile plan or H-plan with a double-pile central range, simply continued with the Netherlandish decorative tradition of the great Jacobean houses

City of London bricklayers developed a distinctive style of their own at this time, especially in the 1630s, e.g. at Kew Palace, London. This loose, eclectic style, often referred to as ARTISAN MANNERISM, emerges elsewhere in the mid C17 in buildings designed by master masons and craftsmen, especially in south-east England where there was an appetite for new houses within the orbit of the capital. It is primarily a style of brick building, and its typical motifs are shaped gables, raised surrounds to the windows, raised quoins or pilasters, pediments of varied design, arches with pronounced voussoirs (wedge-shaped stones), and rustication.

▶ 55. Hull had a strong tradition of brick building, which had begun in the medieval period when the east end of the parish church was rebuilt in this material. Wilberforce House was built 'new from the ground' c. 1660 and is attributed to a local bricklayer, William Catlyn. It displays the repertoire of unorthodox classical motifs associated with the bricklayers of the mid C17, including brickwork laid to emulate rustication

New designs c. 1660–1710

The Restoration of Charles II in 1660 marks a watershed in the architectural history of the house. The king and his reinstated court brought with them from France and Holland new ideas of architectural style, palace planning, gardening and recreation associated with the BAROQUE. This term, originally derogatory, applied to a style which was at its peak in c17 and early c18 Europe. It developed the classical architecture of the Renaissance towards greater extravagance and drama. Its innovations included greater freedom from the conventions of the orders (*see* p. 74), much interplay of concave and convex forms, and a preference for the single visual sweep. After 1660 the King's Office of Works also produced a new generation of educated architects, including Christopher Wren, John Vanbrugh and Nicholas Hawksmoor, who developed a distinctive English version of Continental forms of Baroque architecture. At the same time the end of the Commonwealth saw a new boom in building in the country, akin to the level of activity in the late c16 and early c17 (*see* **The Great Rebuilding**, p. 49). Some of the counties in the north of England (Cumbria, Northumberland, County Durham and Yorkshire) saw the first widespread renewal of many of their houses and this 'Second Great Rebuilding' was as much an urban as a rural phenomenon.

During this period the hipped roof of the mid-century classical houses was suppressed in favour of a consistently horizontal roofline, as at Jones's Queen's House of fifty years earlier (*see* p. 71), but with a swaggering character, sometimes emphasized in the contrasting colours of brick and stone as in Wren's additions to Hampton Court Palace. The most important country houses of this period up to 1700, which express the shift in power from monarch to parliament after the 'Glorious Revolution', are the palaces of powerful landed interests, represented by such mammoth mansions as Chatsworth (Derbys.) by John Talman (completed 1696) and Blenheim (Oxon; begun in 1705) and Castle Howard (North Yorks.; begun 1699), both by John Vanbrugh. All these are one-off commissions by highly individual designers and offer little indication of more general trends. Of course these innovations, as much as the continuation

56. The Folly, Settle, Yorkshire (West Riding), 1670s. The remarkable style of this doorcase is unique to the Pennines. Even at such a late date it combines Gothic motifs with classical ones derived from Serlio

▲　57. Clarendon House, Piccadilly, London, by Sir Roger Pratt, 1664–7

▼　58. Hanbury Hall, Worcestershire, dated 1701. An example of the influence of the style established by Pratt at Clarendon House (above)

of the Italian fashion of the earlier C17 court and London, were largely confined to the nobility and gentry in contact with the metropolis.

One of the first and most influential new designs was Clarendon House, a mansion (demolished) on Piccadilly, London, of 1664–7 by Sir Roger Pratt. This developed the rectangular classical double-pile plan of his Coleshill House into a house-with-wings with a pediment over the three central bays. Belton House, Lincolnshire, begun in 1685, reproduces the design in a slightly modified form and as a formula it proved exceptionally enduring all through the following century for more modest country houses.

Also exceedingly popular among the gentry by the end of the C17 and into the next was the smaller type of house with a rectangular plan and a hipped roof. A good example is Eltham Lodge, on the outskirts of London, designed by Hugh May in 1663 for Sir John Shaw, a banker of great influence at the court of Charles II. It follows the Coleshill pattern in basic terms, but May had travelled in Holland and the use of giant pilasters supporting a central pediment with garlands and coat of arms seems very Dutch. Like

▼ 59. Eltham Lodge, principal front, by Hugh May, 1663–4

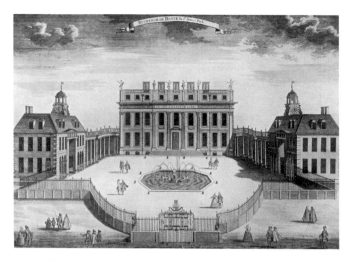

▲ 60. Buckingham House, London, probably by William Winde, 1702–5

Thorpe Hall, Eltham Lodge is a triple pile. Houses like this were being built in Holland in the 1630s. The rectangular plan was equally suited to the growing number of smaller country houses and other later C17 brick houses in the same mode include Ramsbury Manor (Wilts.), Squerryes Court (Kent) and Uppark (West Sussex). The third kind of house plan followed another London trend-setter: Hugh May's Berkeley House (1665), which introduced the formula of a hip-roofed house with quadrant-shaped links to service wings in its forecourt. This pattern was widely adopted among country houses well into the C18, with the wings reserved for the kitchens and stables, or other services.

After 1700 the other highly influential house to be built in London was Buckingham House of 1702–5, probably by William Winde. This had pilasters rising from the ground and a full attic storey instead of a hipped roof. Versions of this formula appear in several places before the end of Queen Anne's reign in houses of various sizes, often reduced to a compact core without wings.

The functions of rooms in a mid- or late C17 country house can be fairly easily summarized and were common across the range from

61. Ince Blundell, Lancashire, by Henry Sephton, c. 1720. The influence of Buckingham House is very clear

large to small. One arrived through the HALL which, depending on size of house, might continue to be a place for reception, or simply an entrance; behind it the saloon was the principal entertaining room, and PARLOURS provided more private family spaces for leisure and eating. They vary in number through the social hierarchy, with a single parlour for the lowliest houses. Bedrooms, or suites of bedroom and withdrawing room, occupy part of the remaining space, usually on the opposite side of the hall and saloon. On the first floor in larger houses would be a dining room and chamber apartments (rooms for the owner and his wife, but also in the largest houses for guests). Royal precedent was important: as in the Elizabethan and Jacobean great houses that anticipated visits from the monarch, the rooms might be arranged to emulate those of the king's palace, with appropriately grand state apartments comprising a sequence of rooms extending either side of the saloon. From the first room, for receiving visitors, these became progressively more private and exclusive, culminating in a bedroom with private closet (or cabinet) (e.g. Ham House, London, 1670s, and Burghley House, Peterborough, 1680s).

▲ 62. Stoneleigh Abbey, Warwickshire, the west range by Francis Smith, 1714–26. This was one of a number of houses Smith designed in the Midlands in the years after 1700, introducing the late Baroque style with its emphasis on height and elevations powerfully framed by giant pilasters. Also very characteristic of this period are the tall windows in each bay and the expression of the middle bay as a centrepiece in which the doorway is linked with the window above

Among houses at the gentry level, many of the innovations introduced in the early to mid C17 were gradually accepted and absorbed, but sometimes over a long time. Lessons in style and planning of houses erected around London may not have been picked up by provincial builders until very much later, and even then perhaps only selectively. So in later C17 houses far from London it is common to find that an interior plan has been brought up to date by adopting a double pile, but externally the style remains loyal to the conservative local traditions of masons and carpenters. Several new farmhouses in the Craven district of Yorkshire's West Riding, for example, persisted with double-storey halls well into the second half of the C17. In the same area occur the remarkable series of carved doorheads which seem to carry on the Gothic style of the medieval period into the later C17 (*see* p. 81). In this respect the VERNACULAR traditions of building in various parts of the country are maintained until *c.* 1700. The varieties of plan forms multiply in middling and smaller houses but there is a move towards symmetry in the new houses of this period, for example in the adoption of a central-passage plan, with a passage between hall and parlour leading to the stair at the rear and chimneys in the end walls. In time the passage becomes a recognizable stair hall of the type very common in the C18.

Other changes in post-Restoration house design can be attributed to the effect of the Great Fire of London in 1666, which destroyed 13,200 houses in the City. The Rebuilding Act of 1667 introduced stricter building regulations and in particular the enforcement of brick facing for new houses to prevent fire (and a minimum thickness for brick walls, with timber only to be used for the frame, doorcases, window frames and cornices). Houses were also graded by size, which was determined by the width of the streets on to which they faced: no more than four storeys were permitted on the main streets.

The result was the TERRACED HOUSE, commonly of three storeys and three bays wide, set over a sunk or semi-sunk basement with an area in front. This became the standard type of dwelling for large and small houses after 1660 and the Rebuilding Act of 1667 served to confirm in legislation what was already accepted as the preferred model. Even outside London, builders and developers began to apply its provisions to new housing. The terraces of Queen Square in Bristol, begun in 1699 when Bristol was establishing itself as the second city after London, were constructed according to building leases that directly emulated the stipulations applied to London buildings as well as something of their character. By the mid C18 many of the London conventions (including those introduced by further Buildings Acts in the early C18) had been accepted as best practice and it is especially noticeable in towns that experienced devastating fires like Warwick in 1694 – an ever-present risk with large numbers of timber-framed buildings.

▲ 63. Nos. 2–3 Essex Court, Temple, London. These are among the few remaining examples of the new type of house built after the Great Fire. They date from 1677 and exhibit several novel features that in time became standard elsewhere. They are brick-faced with stone QUOINS and have horizontal bands dividing the storeys (sometimes known as PLATBANDS). The cornice at roof level has MODILLIONS – the blocks, or consoles, that support the projection of the eaves and which in classical architecture are set along the underside of a Corinthian or Composite order cornice. The windows have keyblocks in the centre of their brick lintels. Another feature common to post-Fire houses in London but also found elsewhere in the late C17 is the coved cornice, a concave curve from the wall-head to the outer edge of the eaves

Details: exteriors

Building in brick offered different options for decoration. FLEMISH BOND, with headers and stretchers alternating in each course, now became the fashion. RUBBED BRICK of a fine red colour was much used from the late C17 to the early C18 as an alternative to stone for window dressings and often combined with cut brick for ornament. Giant pilasters on the façades of Baroque houses in town and country are also often built in brick rather than stone and are either plain or RUSTICATED. Where pilasters are not used they are sometimes implied by raised brick or stone QUOINS at the angles. In the late C17 and early C18 the quoins are often arranged in long-and-short fashion.

The CROSS-WINDOW (*see* p. 78) is the dominant style of window in houses from *c.* 1660 until *c.* 1710. Other Baroque motifs are the oval window, often set vertically, or BULLSEYE (*œil de boeuf*) window. Sliding SASH WINDOWS, composed of two frames set vertically in a box, are thought to have come from Parisian houses, but the introduction of counterbalanced frames operated by cords and pulleys seems to have been one of the innovations introduced by the reinstated court. The earliest surviving example is at Palace House, Newmarket, Suffolk, designed for King Charles II in 1668, and sash windows are known to have been introduced at other royal residences or those of courtiers. They are recorded, for example, at Ham House, London, in 1672–4, as part of improvements made by the Duke and Duchess of Lauder dale, and were used from the outset for Newby Hall, West Riding of Yorkshire, a house just possibly designed by Wren, *c.* 1685–93.

64. Foxdenton Hall, Lancashire, c. 1720, with the early form of sash windows with multiple panes

▲ 65. Rainham Hall, Havering, London, of 1729, is a compact villa beside the Thames between London and Essex. It was a merchant's house, close to his place of business. It exhibits to perfection many of the motifs characteristic of an astylar Baroque house

▼ 66. Terraced houses of c. 1704–5, Queen Anne's Gate, Westminster, London. Note the elaborately carved timber doorcases and the sash windows flush with the wall, features outlawed by later Building Acts

From the early C18 they were beginning to become the standard type in medium and smaller houses. Their size and form varies over time: in the earliest (when the top sash was usually fixed) each frame was divided by thick glazing bars into a grid of squares, sometimes with as many as sixteen lights. By the mid C18 the panes of glass were larger and fewer in number (a six-by-six pattern is common) with slender glazing bars further improving the view and lighting within. However, sash windows were often introduced later, and are not always a reliable guide to a building's date.

As a rule windows of the late C17 and early C18 are straight-headed, but the principal variation is the segmental-headed window (i.e. with a segmental arch head). There are two periods of this fashion in London – post-Restoration and the 1720s–30s – and in the country-side often somewhere between the two. A distinctive early C18 pattern of window LINTEL has bricks cut into a wavy pattern.

Doorcases in this period sometimes have a hood on CONSOLE (curved) BRACKETS, which may be plain or richly carved, e.g. with acanthus leaves. A favourite form for the late C17 and through to the Queen Anne and Early Georgian phase is the arched hood, sometimes with a scallop shell filling the semi-dome over the door. The SWAN-NECK PEDIMENT in which the top of the pediment has a double curve that is broken and ends in scrolls is also a common feature. From the late Baroque phase, but widely used well into the C18, is the GIBBS SURROUND, which has square blocking around the architrave, and is so-called because it is particularly associated with the work of James Gibbs (1682–1754).

Console

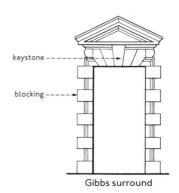

keystone - - - - -

blocking - - - - -▶

Gibbs surround

Details: interiors

PANELLING or wainscotting in C17 houses adopted new and predominantly symmetrical forms, in line with the fashion for external balance. By the late C17 panelling covered the walls of a room and had two or three tiers, with a square panel towards the base of the wall, a vertical and rectangular panel above and perhaps a horizontal rectangle at the top by way of a frieze. In some panelling there will in addition be a chair rail or DADO RAIL; the preoccupation with symmetry may also necessitate placing cupboards to correspond with doors at either end of a wall, or arched niches in the recesses either side of the fireplace; a shell niche with shelves is a familiar motif of the earlier C18. In contrast to Elizabethan and Jacobean styles, panelling is plain, usually RAISED with a moulded edge, and sometimes enriched with carved foliage. In the most important houses this may be accompanied by displays of woodcarving of the Grinling Gibbons school (e.g. Burghley, Chatsworth, and Petworth, West Sussex). Increasingly popular through the late C17 and earli-

▼ 67. Little Grimsby Hall, Lincolnshire, c. 1700, interior

▲ 68. Westwood House, Worcestershire, Great Chamber, ceiling, c. 1670

est years of the C18 is BOLECTION MOULDING, a double curve in profile, which is to be found as much on chimneypieces and doors as on panelling. It is a useful if broad indication of date in house interiors. Raised-and-fielded panelling comes a little later: here the panel is set within the supporting frame and has a bevelled edge around a flat centre. Corner chimneypieces are another late C17 and very early C18 fashion, especially in small rooms within larger houses. In their most lavish form (e.g. at Kensington Palace, Ham House, and Burghley) they have stepped tops intended for the display of china. In smaller houses they are simply set below a section of panelling. Again, the presence of a chimneypiece in this position may be an indication of date for a house or its remodelling.

Fashions for ceilings vary over the course of the mid to late C17. At the Queen's House, Greenwich, Inigo Jones had introduced a new form of timber ceiling divided into compartments by a frame enriched with carved classical decoration (e.g. guilloche) and circular or oval ribs within the frame. By 1637 this style of ceiling is found executed in plasterwork not only at Ham House and in several other houses by followers of Jones (e.g. Coleshill) but also in the remodelled interiors of London merchants' houses up to and including the period of the Commonwealth, with the ribs decorated with fruit and foliage. Late C17 plasterwork is, like the post-Restoration houses

▲ 69. Radclive Manor, Buckinghamshire, C17 staircase, with pierced balustrade, ball pendants and finials

in which it is found, of French and Dutch influence. It employs large wreathed surrounds of, for example, fruit and foliage. From the latest years of the C17 and early C18 painted ceilings and walls became the fashion in wealthier houses, following the precedent set in the royal palaces.

▲ 70. Nos. 98–100 Pilgrim Street, Newcastle, Alderman Fenwick's House, staircase, late C17, with turned balustrades and moulded handrail

In more modest houses the tradition of figurative patterns continued along with decoration that imitated textiles, wall hangings and panelling. Polychrome painting became more affordable in this period and there is a remarkable scheme in the Merchants House, Marlborough, Wilts, of the late C17 with vertical rainbow stripes.

The decoration of staircases in the C17 varies over time, with BALUSTERS of various forms – turned, flat or splat (cut from a flat section giving the outline of a baluster shape and thus cheaper) – and BALUSTRADES that might be pierced (e.g. with carved trophies at Ham House) or elaborately carved scrolls (e.g. Thorpe Hall, *c.* 1675, and Dunster Castle, Somerset, *c.* 1685) or geometric patterns. A favoured later C17 type is the turned baluster with a pronounced belly (e.g. Alderman Fenwick's House, Newcastle), or the Italianate type with foliage around the base. Also to be associated with the early C17 Palladian style, and again widely used in its revival in the early C18 (see p. 134), is the vertically symmetrical baluster. Spiral or twisted balusters appear in the late C17 and continue in use into the early C18. Moulded handrails give way to ones of wide, flat appearance by the early C18.

THE GEORGIAN HOUSE, c. 1710–1830

The division in the Georgian period remains between on the one hand developments in country houses, spurred on by increasing land values across much of the country, and on the other the growing demand from the same aristocratic and gentry class for new houses in the cities and towns. In London, parliament fuelled the requirement for residences in its proximity when it was in session, and further promoted speculative development on open land. The social life of the 'season' in the summer months encouraged major developments of temporary, and later permanent, residences in the new resorts – first at Bath and subsequently at Brighton, Buxton, Cheltenham and Leamington – and for the gentry in the county towns. By the early C19 the growing middle classes involved in commerce and industry were beginning to prove influential in house design.

Early and mid-Georgian planning and design

The Baroque style continued to be fashionable well into the C18 in the provinces, and as always the preference continued for longer among gentry and lesser houses. The years around 1720 saw a revival of the strict style of PALLADIANISM, conceived as a direct counter to what its adherents perceived as Baroque's corrupting influence on English architecture since the time of Inigo Jones. This was not just a matter of taste: it was also one of politics. Crudely speaking Baroque was tainted as foreign, a Catholic style associated with the Tory supporters of King Charles II and his brother, James II. With the latter's overthrow in 1688 in favour of the Protestant William of Orange and the Hanoverian succession in 1714, the rival Whig party triumphed as the representatives of the national interest.

◀   71. Camden Crescent, Bath, by John Eveleigh, 1788

▲   72. Wanstead House, Essex, by Colen Campbell, begun in 1715

In architecture the promoters of the new style sought to return to the principles of Vitruvius, as espoused in the c16 by Palladio, whose *Quattro Libri* ('Four Books of Architecture', 1570) were translated into English for the first time by the architect Giacomo Leoni in 1715. In the same year, the architect Colen Campbell published *Vitruvius Britannicus*, providing the first proper survey of contemporary and recent architecture in the classical tradition. Elevations and plans of major houses of the Baroque generation by Talman, Vanbrugh, Hawksmoor and Thomas Archer were included, but also among the engravings was Campbell's own design for Wanstead House, built for Sir Richard Child in the Essex countryside close to London's eastern edge.

Wanstead House established the pattern for the grand Georgian country house. It expresses all the values associated with Palladianism: mathematical proportions and a hierarchy which distinguished between a RUSTICATED BASEMENT, an entrance at the level of the PIANO NOBILE reached by an external double staircase, windows and doorways with PEDIMENTS (alternating segmental and triangular), and an ATTIC with square windows. Wanstead also had a six-column (hexastyle) PORTICO. This feature, resulting in the so-called 'temple front' (*see* also p. 72), was assumed incorrectly by Palladio to have been a defining characteristic of Roman villas. The Palladians, led by Richard Boyle, 3rd Earl of Burlington (1694–1753), adopted it without question. Like Inigo Jones a century before, Burlington had visited Italy in 1715 and 1719 to acquaint himself at

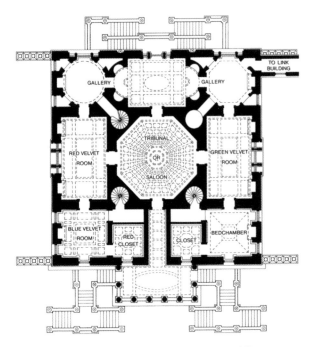

Labels within plan: TO LINK BUILDING, GALLERY, GALLERY, TRIBUNAL, RED VELVET ROOM, GREEN VELVET ROOM, SALOON, BLUE VELVET ROOM, RED CLOSET, CLOSET, BEDCHAMBER

▲ 73. Chiswick House, plan of the principal floor

first hand with Palladio's villas and applied his knowledge to the design of his villa at Chiswick, west of London, in 1727–9. This was a 'small but splendid recreation of the antique spirit' loosely modelled on Palladio's Villa Rotonda (and the Villa Pisani, designed by Vincenzo Scamozzi, Palladio's successor in Vicenza).

The centralized square plan of Chiswick House with all rooms on the ground and first floors orbiting around an octagonal hall, derives in part from Inigo Jones's Queen's House at Greenwich (p. 70). Although the compact layout is different from the great spreading plans of the Baroque houses, the essential hierarchy of a sequence of rooms ending in a private closet is as before. At Palladian country houses like Wanstead the earlier practice continued of a central hall and saloon with suites of apartments extending outwards to fill wings of prodigious length. In both versions the kitchen and services could be set in the basement, or more commonly banished to pavilion wings that were linked to the central core by quadrant passages (cf. Berkeley House, p. 84). In the very largest houses like Holkham in Norfolk, built for the Earl of Leicester in the 1730s, there were no fewer than four wings, including one for the accommodation of guests.

Few houses were built either on a scale comparable with Wanstead or as purely Palladian as Chiswick, but Campbell and Burlington's followers – notably William Kent, who published *The Designs of Inigo Jones* in 1727, Roger Morris, Isaac Ware (who produced his own translation of Palladio in 1738 and *A Complete Body of Architecture* in 1756–7), Henry Flitcroft, James Paine and John Carr – applied the same values to houses of varying size. By the mid c18 Palladianism had become the orthodoxy of design for innumerable houses large and small.

The Palladian interior was conceived as a series of spaces whose dimensions were dictated by a system of harmonious proportions. In terms of decoration and fittings, pure Palladian interiors in

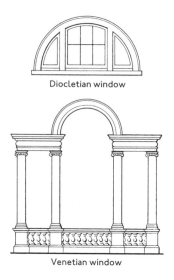

Diocletian window

Venetian window

▲ 74. Two key classical motifs reintroduced to domestic architecture at Chiswick House

75. Hagley Hall, Worcestershire (1754–60), by Sanderson Miller; one of a number of Palladian country houses to adopt the compact plan and appearance of Houghton Hall, Norfolk, designed by James Gibbs and Colen Campbell for Sir Robert Walpole in 1722. The motif of corner towers with pyramid roofs dates back to Wilton House, Wiltshire, designed in the 1630s

76. The Gallery ceiling, Chiswick House, London, by William Kent, c. 1727–38

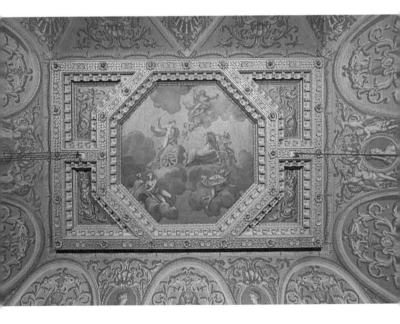

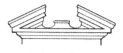

Broken pediment

Segmental pediment

Swan-neck pediment

country houses are considerably more opulent than their restrained elevations imply. Palladio provided little detailed guidance for the decoration of interiors, so the style was largely evolved by his English followers, especially William Kent, Lord Burlington's collaborator at Chiswick and Holkham. Ceilings follow the compartmented form first introduced by Jones at Whitehall Palace's Banqueting House and the Queen's House, Greenwich (*see* p. 80). Lord Burlington's house at Chiswick, designed by Kent, had a COFFERED ceiling over the central 'tribune', derived from the Basilica of Maxentius in Rome.

Following the principles of design set out by Inigo Jones a century before the Palladian inspired houses of this time also adopted the low-pitched and hipped style of roofs, which were necessary in classical houses without gables and which could be made almost invisible behind the parapet or balustrade. Kingpost and queenpost roof trusses (*see* p. 35) especially suited these wider spanning and shallower types of roof and could be constructed with a flat section in place of a ridge or an M-type omitting the ridge altogether. These forms of truss are the dominant ones in houses from this period forward. Palladian doorcases are usually pedimented, in both 'open' and 'broken' forms, or with a flat cornice raised on an upswept frieze. Popular motifs are the KEY PATTERN and the VITRUVIAN SCROLL.

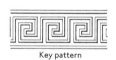

Key pattern

Vitruvian scroll

THE VILLA

By the second half of the C18 the most popular type of country residence was the villa. This was either a secondary seat to the main estate of its owner or, and more commonly from the late C17 with the expansion of London, a residence within easy distance of a city for a merchant or other city dweller or simply for gentlemen without fortunes. The Home Counties ringing London and along the Thames are exceptionally rich in this type of small dwelling. Many of the best are by Sir Robert Taylor and in such houses the number of rooms is reduced to an essential group of hall, saloon, drawing room and library. It remained the middle-class ideal well into the C19.

▲ 77. Clifton Hill House, Bristol, by Isaac Ware, 1746–50, is an exemplar of the Palladian merchant's villa, built for a local draper. The composition of this front is similar to the Villa Ragona at Le Ghizzole by Palladio, whose *Quattro Libri* Ware had published in English in 1738

Early to mid-eighteenth-century town houses

Although most wealth was concentrated in the hands of the aristocracy and gentry who led the boom in country house building, England in the C18 experienced rapid population growth, from about six and a half million *c.* 1750 to nine million inhabitants by 1801. By the later date, a million people lived in London alone and tens of thousands in the other towns such as Birmingham, Bristol, Liverpool and Manchester that had burgeoned during the industrial revolution. For this period, the subject of houses in towns and cities becomes increasingly important, as does the role of town planning to accommodate the growing population in residences of appropriate quality. By the early years of the C19 new house types were appearing in towns: the semi-detached house and the detached suburban villa sprang up as the growing middle class abandoned congested towns for a semi-rural existence.

▼   78. Prince Street, Hull. Terraces of eighteenth-century housing

The planned developments of housing in terraces and squares which emerged in London, Bath and elsewhere in the C18 was due to a change in the way that housing speculators operated. London after the Great Fire heralded the way, with builders leasing parcels of ground from the landowner at a fixed rent ('ground rent') and bearing the cost of erecting the houses themselves in the hope of selling or renting them once complete. The landlords could control the architectural appearance of the developments on their property through conditions known as covenants. These could also specify the type of housing to be built, the use to which it could be put, and the materials for construction.

By the later C18 the standard term of the lease, after which it 'fell-in' and reverted to the landowner who could then increase the ground rent, was ninety-nine years. This encouraged builders to invest in houses of better life expectancy. In parts of London that were initially developed on shorter leases of about thirty or forty years, the houses were replaced with ones of higher standard once the term of the original lease had expired.

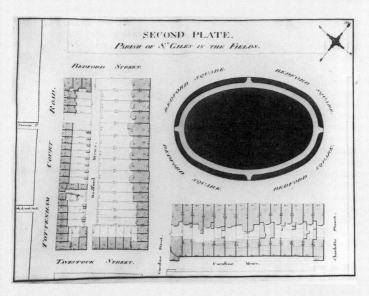

79. Bedford Square, Bloomsbury, London. Plan of the layout of terraced houses on the west and south sides of the square with its oval private garden. This remains one of the best-preserved examples of speculative development in late C18 London

▲ 80. General Wade's House, Bath. Built c. 1720, a good example of the persistenc
of Baroque styles of urban house elevation into the first quarter of the C18

81. No. 76 Brook Street, Mayfair, London, by Colen Campbell, c. 1720. Horizontal mouldings imply the base and entablature of a giant order but the pilaster is omitted

The predominant urban form continued to be the TERRACED HOUSE. The Palladian revival generally involved subjecting the proportions of the front elevations to an implied order rising through the first and second floors, with the ground floor visually treated as a basement. The first floor, as in the great house the *piano nobile*, is taller than the second, in contrast to the typical post-Great Fire of London terrace which had ground, first and second floors of matching height. Windows become smaller in relation to the wall, and the absent order is often signalled by horizontal mouldings.

A useful comparison between a fully fledged late Baroque urban front of *c.* 1720 and one of almost exactly contemporary date but exhibiting Palladian principles is between General Wade's House in Bath (l.) and a house (now demolished) at No.76 Brook Street, Mayfair, London (above). Needless to say, although London houses were starting to exhibit Palladian features it is quite normal to find the late C17 type of house façade continuing in provincial towns for decades longer.

The next step was to group the individual façades into a larger, single composition, which came to be known as the palace front. The idea goes back to Inigo Jones in Covent Garden in the 1630s (*see* p. 71) and in the early C18 an aborted attempt by Campbell to build in a unified way in his new Grosvenor Square, London. But the concept flourished quickly in the fast-developing resort town of Bath, which from 1725 set the architectural fashion for England. The great innovation was made in Queen Square by John Wood in 1728–36,

▲ 82. Queen Square, Bath, watercolour by T. Malton Jun (1784) of the north and west sides showing a terrace with a 'palace front'

the north side of which is one composition of twenty-three bays, with the centre five emphasized by an engaged pediment and attached columns; the end three bays also have engaged columns as well as a full attic above the cornice. The palace front is developed further in the sequence of planned streets that include the Circus, where curved terraces create a complete enclosure around a garden. There the continuity of elevation is created by columns set in pairs on each storey and framing each bay of the façade. In the Royal Crescent the first and second floors are encompassed by a giant Ionic order. The placing of the best rooms on the *piano nobile* and the view from within across the landscape set these terraces on the level of the country house and made the urban terrace acceptable to the nobility.

By the early C18 the interior plan of TERRACED HOUSES of two- or three-bay fronts had become more or less standardized, with the staircase placed at the back of the narrow entrance hall – sometimes with an arch spanning the width of the entrance hall – and fireplaces positioned in the party walls between the houses. To one side of the entrance hall would be the dining room, with a parlour behind that. In keeping with Palladian principles the *piano nobile* is at first-floor level and comprises a large drawing room occupying the whole of the front and a smaller drawing room immediately behind at right angles. On the second floor are the principal bedrooms. The attic, its roof partly concealed from the street by the front parapet, was for servants and children, and the basement contained the kitchen and other services.

▲ 83. A model of a late c18 house in Great Pulteney Street, Bath, showing the arrangement of the interior spaces of the larger class of terraced house, distributed over six floors from cellars to attic. The placing of the stair alongside a smaller rear room on each floor was space efficient and became the standard type of plan in terraces large and small

84. Design for an entablature from Batty Langley's *Gothick Architecture Improved* (1741–2)

The amount of time spent by the upper classes in London and the spa towns like Bath each year, and by county gentry in the major county towns (such as Nottingham, Newcastle, York and Norwich), was important for carrying back to the country the latest fashions in house design. There were already by the later C17 manuals to instruct carpenters in all aspects of the construction of floors, roofs and staircases but from the early C18 it also became much easier for provincial architects, masons, builders and craftsmen to copy these fashions for their clients with the assistance of **pattern books**.

An early precedent is *A Book of Architecture*, published in 1728 by James Gibbs, an architect with feet in both the Baroque and Palladian camps. This volume showcased his own designs but also included plates of fittings such as chimneypieces, thereby making it useful to a broader audience in need of sources for their designs. Over about twenty years from the mid 1720s a large number of manuals of this type were issued by Batty Langley (1696–1751) as a practical aid, especially to understanding and executing classical and Gothic styles of architecture. Any mention of a feature 'copied from Batty Langley' refers to these manuals. Other widely used volumes were Abraham Swan's *The British Architect, or, The Builder's Treasury …* (1757) and William Pain's *Practical Builder* (1774).

Georgian and Regency styles

By the mid c18 the panoply of classical motifs of columns, pilasters, pediments and Venetian windows found in the great houses had filtered down to medium and small ones. In the second half of the c18, however, a younger generation of architects sought a more detailed understanding of the architecture of classical Antiquity, rather than the view presented to them by Palladio, Jones and Lord Burlington. The results have come to be called NEOCLASSICISM, but this catch-all term obscures much variety and complexity. To summarize its effects on houses, however, externally they have a greater plainness and severity and their decoration is thinner and more delicately handled. This was the era of the Grand Tour, the formation of great collections of antiquities, and more detailed archaeological excavation of, among other sites, the ruins of Rome, Pompeii and Herculaneum. Publication of the newly discovered objects and paintings established a wider decorative vocabulary for classical Antiquity. Further discoveries by architectural travellers were published in volumes such as *The Ruins of Palmyra* (1753) and *The Ruins of Baalbec* (1757), both by James Woods, and *The Ruins of the Palace of the Emperor Diocletian at Spalatro* (1764) by Robert Adam. Robert Adam stands out as the leading innovator, drawing on multiple Antique sources for his style and the ingenuity of his interior planning, with rooms that are by turn apse-ended, circular and octagonal, and are decorated in patterns derived from the styles of ornament found at Herculaneum and Pompeii, among other places. His style, though frowned upon by many contemporaries, was quickly taken up by other architects, builders and decorators and became the default mode for decoration in many of the new developments in London.

At the same time there was a renewed interest in the GOTHIC style of medieval architecture, although less in the design and appearance of medieval houses and more in their decorative vocabulary. It initially found favour as a style for garden buildings and sham ruins, or in, for example, Vanbrugh's castellated style of house. Even the Palladians were not averse to employing Gothic motifs for incidents in the landscape (James Gibbs designed his Gothick Temple in the grounds of Stowe, Buckinghamshire, in the 1740s).

85. Moccas Court, Herefordshire by Anthony Keck. Begun 1776, circular drawing room with ceiling by Robert Adam, 1781, wall decoration of 1790

Just as Lord Burlington was the champion of Palladian classicism as a national style, so Horace Walpole (1717–97) became the leading promoter of the taste for Gothic as a style uniquely rooted in England's pre-Reformation past. Strawberry Hill, his own house at Twickenham on the Thames, was designed in partnership with his closest acquaintances – known subsequently as the 'Committee of Taste' – who included the amateur architect John Chute and the designer Richard Bentley. This phase of the Gothic Revival is usually referred to as GOTHICK and was at its peak *c.* 1730–80. It is marked by thin delicate forms used without much regard for archaeological

86. Donnington Grove, Berkshire, by John Chute, 1763. View of the staircase

▲   87. Blue Drawing Room, St Michael's Mount, Cornwall, late 1740s, demonstrating the co-habitation of Gothick and Rococo styles of interior decoration

accuracy or structural logic, being more concerned with Romantic
atmosphere, famously represented by such extravagant follies as
Fonthill Abbey, Wiltshire, by James Wyatt (1746–1813). There were at
this time no studies of medieval buildings equivalent to those available to architects working in the classical tradition. Among the earliest publications was *The Ancient Architecture of England* (1795–1814)
by the architect and draughtsman John Carter.

The Gothic Revival of the c18 emphasized asymmetry in plan
and elevation and left a legacy in the varied character of small cottages and villas built in suburban and rural situations under the
influence of the PICTURESQUE movement (*see* p. 120). It also
found expression in the revival among country houses of a castle
style, especially during the period of the Napoleonic Wars as an
assertion of national identity and resistance. Confusingly many

88. Brighton Pavilion, w front, 1786–1822. A house that grew from cottage to villa to palace. Its progressive enlargement for the Prince of Wales, beginning in 1786 and culminating in 1822, epitomises the breadth of late C18 and early C19 architectural and decorative styles beginning with French Neoclassicism, via *chinoiserie* and ending in picturesque evocations of India's Mughal architecture

89. Egypt Corner, Northwood House, Cowes, Isle of Wight, by George J.J. Mair, c. 1836–7

such houses that sport battlements, arrow loops and other motifs of medieval castle architecture are nevertheless entirely symmetrical. In the hands of architects like Robert Adam, they might also have interiors with Neoclassical decoration. Gothick is frequently associated with the ROCOCO (a decorative style characterized by asymmetrical ornament) and CHINOISERIE (from 'chinois', the French for Chinese) two of the many decorative options available to designers of interiors in the 1740s to 1780s. At the end of the 1780s knowledge of Indian styles of architecture was spread by William Hodges's *Views of India* (1786) and *Views of Oriental Scenery* by Thomas and William Daniels (from 1795). The effect is best represented in the domes of the Prince's Regent's playhouse, the Brighton Pavilion (*see* fig. 88), as remodelled by Nash in 1815–22. The last contribution to the revival of the architecture of Antiquity is the Egyptian, which came into fashion thanks to the records of buildings brought back during and after Napoleon's campaigns. Its impact on houses is primarily restricted to interiors, such as the dining room at Goodwood House, West Sussex.

The publication of three volumes on the *Antiquities of Athens* (1762, 1787 and 1794) by James Stuart and Nicholas Revett inspired the GREEK REVIVAL. Greece, as part of the Ottoman Empire, was harder to reach as a tourist but gradually became part of the Grand Tour in the later C18, especially once Italy was put out of reach by the Napoleonic Wars. Studies of Greek architecture and decoration introduced around 1760 the varied forms of the baseless GREEK DORIC order, with its distinctive flared profile, fluted or unfluted column and large plain capital, the GREEK IONIC order as it appeared in the Erectheion, and the CORINTHIAN ORDER (*see* p. 75). Unsurprisingly once again it was in garden buildings – the little temples set into the landscapes

Anthemion and Palmette

around country houses – that the Greek style was first taken up.

The purity of Greek classicism and its emphasis on form rather than ornament was admired and was also regarded as well-suited to civic architecture such as museums and town halls. The Greek cause in its War of Independence from the Turks also strengthened the

▲ 90. The Grange, Northington, Hampshire, by William Wilkins, 1809–10, is a mansion posing as a Doric temple set in parkland. Many smaller houses also favoured the spare outline and thin detail of the Grecian style without aiming to be as archaeological as The Grange; the style is much more often found among smaller country and suburban villas than in great houses

Greek Revival, which in the period *c.* 1790–1840 resulted in a series of austere country houses either with porticos or deriving their power from a concentration on spare, cubic forms. The principal figures in this fashion include Robert Smirke, George Dance, William Wilkins, C. R. Cockerell, John Dobson and J. P. Gandy as well as the very original style of Sir John Soane. Key motifs are the ANTHE-MION (ornament based on honeysuckle flowers and leaves) and the wreath. A style of capital often encountered is the one recorded on the C2 B.C. TOWER OF THE WINDS, with acanthus leaves and palm leaves set vertically.

▲ 91. Wimpole Hall, Book Room, by Sir John Soane, begun 1791, demonstrates this architect's sense of spatial adventure and sparing of detail

THE PICTURESQUE

The Picturesque is an approach to architecture and landscape design first defined in the later c18 by English theorists, notably Sir Uvedale Price and Richard Payne Knight. Widely influential on gardens and parks in the late c18 and early c19, it is characterized in architecture by irregular forms and textures, sometimes with the implication of gradual growth or decay. The scenic manner of composing buildings in a landscape was closely related to the paintings of Claude (c. 1600–1682) and Nicolas Poussin (1594–1665). Although that might suggest a preference for Italian styles of building, the quintessential expression of the Picturesque is the cottage orné, with rustic timber columns made from bark-covered tree trunks and tiled or thatched roofs with carved bargeboards. It is applied predominantly in small rural villas, parsonages and estate cottages. Early c19 pattern books such as P. F. Robinson's *Rural Architecture* (1828) and J. B. Papworth's *Rural Residences* (1818, 2nd ed. 1832) offered builders a rich choice of model designs in Swiss, Gothic, Tudor and other styles. To give his clients an idea of how their house and garden might look after reorganization on Picturesque principles, Humphry Repton produced his 'Red Books' with 'before' and 'after' views.

92. Blaise Hamlet, near Bristol. Designed in 1810–11 by John Nash, with George Repton, as a place of retirement for workers on the Harford estate. It is the *nec plus ultra* of picturesque layout and design

Later Georgian urban developments

As England's cities and towns burgeoned in the era of industriali-
zation, the terrace was triumphant as the home of the many. The
London Building Act of 1774 divided TERRACED HOUSES into a
hierarchy of four types or 'rates' – first-, second-, third- and fourth-
rate – with prescriptions for their design, and introduced better forms of supervision of standards by local surveyors. Between
about 1790 and 1840, broadly speaking the REGENCY PERIOD,
the scale and ambition of urban planning achieved a new order of
grandeur. The standard layout, following classical principles, is the

93. Albert Gardens, Commercial Road, Stepney, London. Medium-size terraces
of the early C19 in the East End of London. They emulate grander West End
developments in the formal layout around a square but without any emphasis
in the elevations to create a classical composition. The recessed round arched
doors and windows are typical of housing after the 1774 Building Act (see p.128).
The boxes of the sash windows (by now a standard six-over-six pattern) are fully
rebated within brickwork for fire protection

square surrounded by service streets, and several of the newly developed estates in London of this period conform to this pattern. The influence spread during the same period to places like Brighton, Hastings, Cheltenham, Leamington and Newcastle.

There were also developments in planning inside the larger late c18 and early c19 town houses. From about 1750, especially in the major London houses where entertainment was now the main activity, the plan evolved to create a circuit of rooms on the first floor round a central staircase, aiding the movement of visitors in an uninterrupted sequence into, up, around, down and out. Changing patterns of decoration and even the shape of the rooms – octagons, squares, ovals – lent variety and richness to the experience. The priority given to social activity also signals another change to be noted

▲ 94. Semi–detached house on the Lloyd Baker Estate, Islington, London, built 1833. Two houses share a common elevation to the street unified by a pediment Entrances are placed at the side or in single–storey links between the pairs

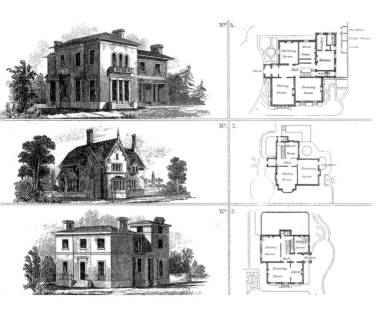

95. Tunbridge Wells, Calverley Park villas, perspectives and plans by J. Britton, 1832

in both town and country houses: the introduction of the dining room as one of the grandest interiors.

Contemporary with new developments there was also much rebuilding and in particular refacing of older buildings in smaller towns, for example concealing timber-framed buildings on narrow plots behind new and wider symmetrical brick façades. Smaller terraced houses continued to follow the pattern of their earlier C18 superiors, with entrance into a passage to the stair and a single room front and back. A notable change in the smaller terrace of the early C19 is that it is no longer possible to maintain symmetry on the ground floor: the door and single window for the front room are no longer aligned with the two windows of the first floor.

A new domestic type at this time was the semi-detached house, in which two dwellings are joined by a party wall to create a symmetrical whole, sometimes emphasized by a shared pediment. In the Regency period it is common to see a type in which the pairs of houses have their entrances in a bay to the side, sometimes joined to the next pair in the group. But the growing urban middle class was increasingly devoted to the detached VILLA, set in its own garden or modest grounds, away from the congested centre. John Nash in his development of the Park Villages around Regent's Park, London, in the early C19 demonstrated that villas could be designed in any number of styles, from Greek to Gothic, Tudor to Italianate. The villa suburbs designed in the early C19 by Decimus Burton at, for example, Calverley Park, Tunbridge Wells, Kent, and St Leonards on Sea, East Sussex, show the same stylistic variety. Many adopted the appearance of a toy fort with battlements, or a *cottage orné* with rustic porches, verandas and Gothick windows, declaring their affiliation with rural traditions and disquiet with urban life.

At the same time the demands of supplying the urban centres were answered by agricultural improvement in the countryside and the associated enclosure of land, resulting in the building of new farmhouses, rectories, etc. Even at this level the classical influence can be detected in houses of more or less square plan with a central doorway into an entrance hall, a room on either side, and kitchen and service rooms in the rear pile or in a wing at the back.

Georgian details: exteriors

One of the first things to note in Georgian houses is the disappearance of timber as a significant element in their external elevations. By 1700 supplies of wood for framing were almost entirely exhausted in England, and from this time stone took over for middling and smaller houses in those areas where it could be quarried nearby, for example the limestones in the belt running between Lincolnshire and Somerset and in the far northern counties, or the sandstones prevalent in parts of Lancashire, Yorkshire and to a lesser extent in parts of Hampshire, Surrey and Sussex. Stone was used either as the masonry of the walls or simply as a facing over rubble or brick. The classical influence in the C18 gave stone a cachet above other materials. Nevertheless, it was expensive to quarry and work and so away from the stone areas it was an option only for grander houses. In parts of the downland areas of the South-East and East Anglia much use was made of flints extracted from the chalk, either as complete nodules or cut ('knapped').

In London and the South-East, the revolution in transport – notably canals – by the early C19 made it much easier to export BRICK and other materials across the country. Colours of brick

▲　96. Shermans, Dedham, Essex. A house of c. 1601, refronted in 1730–1.
A fine example of the effect to be achieved with contrasting brick
colours, here a mixture of red and the pale yellow bricks made from
gault clay. Another popular variation of the earlier C18 is blue-grey bricks
contrasted with dressings of red or mixed into a chequered pattern

vary from one part of the country to another – yellow in London,
red in the southern counties and the north of England and distinctive pale bricks, ranging from white to grey, in East Anglia. To
overcome the problem of handmade bricks having rough edges,
bricklayers devised techniques such as tuckpointing – a thin raised

▲ 97. John Soane's Museum, Lincoln's Inn Fields. Remodelled by Sir John Soane from three standard late C18 terraced houses, No.13 (centre) is stone-faced with incised decoration in a Grecian style and topped by caryatids made of Coade stone. At the top balustrade are forms of acroteria

strip of mortar laid between the bricks to give the impression of precise jointing. In towns which suffered devastating fires, new buildings were almost always in brick (even in stone regions), and in many other places it became quite usual for timber-framed buildings to be encased in brick or refaced on the street elevation to hide the frame. Another solution, virtually confined to the east and south-east of England, was TILE-HANGING – setting clay tiles vertically and overlapping on the face and sides of a framed building. Interlocking MATHEMATICAL TILES, which emulate brickwork so well that it is often hard to distinguish the two, are a refinement of this. A very grand example of their use is Althorp, Northamptonshire *c.* 1786–90 but they are mostly found in vernacular buildings of the south-eastern counties from *c.* 1725 onwards. An alternative in modest houses is WEATHERBOARDING with horizontal overlapping boards, which was as much a feature of the rural areas in the south and east of England as smaller C18 urban houses in parts of London, or SLATE HANGING (especially in Devon and Cornwall).

Some materials are new to the late C18 and early C19. STUCCO is a durable lime plaster, sometimes incorporating marble dust. It had long been used in interiors for ornamental or architectural features. Externally, as a protective coating it offered a clear benefit to classical houses built in areas lacking good stone. By the early C19 it was possible to give even quite modest brick-built houses the appearance of fine stone. Lines could be drawn in the stucco to imitate ashlar or rustication, and in the era of the Greek Revival ornament is sometimes restricted to incised lines of decoration, on pilasters for example (e.g. John Soane's Museum, Lincoln's Inn Fields, London). The best examples of stucco houses are in the London developments by John Nash for the Prince Regent comprising Carlton Palace, Regent Street and the buildings around the new Regent's Park, as well as the fashionable resort towns of this period such as Cheltenham and especially Brighton. COADE STONE, a form of ceramic artificial cast stone, was made in Lambeth by Eleanor Coade (d.1821) and her associates. It provided a wide range of ornamental mouldings and decorations in every style for application to houses and was much favoured by Robert Adam to achieve a richer ornamentation for the façades of his houses.

Up to 1750 doorcases frequently have engaged columns or pilasters and a pediment. A version which in London can be dated quite accurately to *c.* 1720–30 has a frieze with an upswept cornice. After 1750 a popular type is the arched fanlight rising into an OPEN PEDIMENT supported on columns or half-columns. In London the 1774 Building Act further restricted the use of external timberwork and although wooden doorcases were still permitted, a new type of round-arched doorway recessed into the wall developed. A lavish version is that with

▲ 98. Buckingham Street, London, early C18 doorcase

▼ 99. Bedford Square, Bloomsbury, 1775–83. The door arches in Bedford Square are given raised and moulded rusticated voussoirs made of Coade Stone (*see* p. 127)

a wide arched fanlight over a tripartite doorcase with sidelights flanking the door. It is the form used at Bedford Square, Bloomsbury, London, laid out in 1775–83, the first square in London to achieve complete uniformity of design with palace front terraces around all four sides.

In the Regency period doorcases surrounded by REEDING (narrow vertical mouldings like bundles of reeds) are commonplace, along with FANLIGHTS of umbrella, batwing and teardrop patterns.

A greater proportion of the wall space of Late Georgian and Regency houses is given to windows. The London Building Act of 1774 introduced a regulation which required the boxes of sash windows to be rebated behind the brickwork of the window openings, and this precaution against fire was taken up elsewhere over time. First-floor windows in urban housing of the late C18 and early C19 are often carried to the floor, to provide as much light as possible

▼ 100. Brunswick Square, Brighton, by Charles Busby, c. 1825. The grandest expression of the fashion for bows

to the principal living room. Towards 1800 and after, these windows are often framed by arches, so breaking up the wall surface further. Ironwork balconies or BALCONETTES become a standard feature in many Late Georgian London houses and soon appear elsewhere. The Regency period favoured balconies with tent-like canopies and trellis-patterns, but in detail such ironwork varies from the light Neoclassicsim of Adam to Grecian motifs and Gothick patterns. After *c.* 1730 BAY WINDOWS are a new form that was designed to enhance the view from inside. At first of CANTED shape (with angled edges or sides), they had evolved into BOW WINDOWS (curved) by the mid C18. As so often, the innovation was made in the speculative developments in London and Bath and by the early C19 had spread to Brighton, Cheltenham and other fashionable resorts. OGEE-HEADED (with double curves) and pointed sash windows, in which INTERSECTING glazing bars at the head imitate tracery, are a particular feature of the Gothick phase of *c.* 1730–80.

Houses of the later C18 and early C19 have roofs of lower pitch, especially where light slates and PANTILES are used as the covering. Local traditions for roofing were kept to in most areas (e.g. slate roofs in the Lakeland areas and stone flags and tiles in the limestone belt and Pennines), but Welsh slates were in widespread use from about 1760, first in the new developments of Georgian London and elsewhere thereafter. The most common form of roof is the hipped roof, but in terraces in particular the roof pitches are hidden by a parapet.

Georgian details: interiors

Styles of PANELLING in higher status houses change in the earlier C18 from all-over type with bolection moulding to one in which,as outside, the basic division of the classical order if followed – with dado for plinth, wall surface for column, and cornice for antablature. The style of panelling becomes plainer in this period and as the C18 century progresses it is increasingly uncommon for the wall to be panelled above the dado, leaving a plaster box cornice to continue to define the order.

101. Royal Fort House, Bristol. Rococo doorcase in the dining room, early 1760s

The empty space of the wall was thus free for other forms of decoration in the most expensive houses. Plasterwork for walls and ceilings was much in vogue in the middle of the C18 with the fashion *c.* 1750-60 for Rococo forms of decoration, with scrolls, shellwork and patterns of ornament often in C- or S-shapes (papier mache was a cheaper alternative to plaster). It was also the vehicle for creating the elaborate fan-vaulting and other details required by interiors in a Gothick style. Under the Neoclassical influence plasterwork changes to low-relief geometric patterns of circles, semicircles, squares and octagons decorated with gryphons, urns, swags, garlands, anthemion

◄ 102. Edgbaston Hall
Birmingham, stair-
case by William and
David Hiorn, 1751–2

▲ 103. No. 7 Great George Street, Bristol, study, by William Paty, 1788–91

▶ 104. Pompeian Room, Hinxton Hall, Cambridgeshire, c. 1830

and palmettes, enriched by highly coloured and gilded painting. The fashion for Pompeiian styles of painting, resulted in rooms finished in vivid blocks of colour.

More generally painting walls in a single colour could be used to stress the classical division of the wall surface by applying contrasting colours to the skirting, dado, wall, cornice etc. and by the early C19 painters were also able to create effects of marbling and graining to imitate wood. Silk hangings were the preserve of the wealthy and so was printed wallpaper which was taxed from 1712 until 1836. Stencilling was a cheaper alternative for many smaller house interiors.

For columns and pilasters in the Neoclassical phase there is an increase in the use of either marbles or SCAGLIOLA, the composite stone made from coloured marble dust, and by no means a cheaper alternative to marble itlsef.

By the early C18 staircases are much more likelt to be CANTI-LEVERED from the wall and have an OPEN STRING, i.e. with the profile of the treads and risers of the staircase revealed, and carved with scrolls on their ends - a decorative feature which dies out after *c.* 1750. Grander staircases of this period commonly have three balusters per tread. sometimes combinations of twisted and fluted balusters. In the mid C18 column balusters progressively supersede them and become more and more elogated, until the stick baluster takes

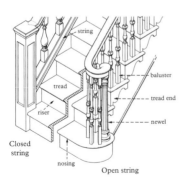

string

baluster

tread

tread end

riser

newel

Closed string

nosing

Open string

over *c.* 1770. It is not uncommon to find the latest form of baluster used in the main staircase and an earlier mode for the backstair or the flight to the attic, seen only by servants. London and Bath houses are unusual in having stone staircases and by the mid C18 metal balustrades of S-scrolls or lyre patterns.

VICTORIAN AND EDWARDIAN HOUSES
1837–1910

It would be easy to be overwhelmed by the sheer quantity and variety of housing in Victorian England. This was a period not only of rapid expansion in cities and towns of every size but also the building and rebuilding of large country houses. The picture is made even more confusing by the fact that it is very difficult to follow developments chronologically, as new styles and techniques appear simultaneously.

Styles and motifs

Before saying something about the different types and classes of house and their details it is worth noting the proliferation of historic styles, running in parallel and applied across a range of house types of each social class. The peak of the CLASSICAL TRADITION comes with the ITALIANATE. Largely based on the style of Renaissance *palazzi* or Tuscan farmhouses instead of the Antique Roman and Greek classicism favoured by a previous generation, it is a style that was given the seal of approval by its choice for Osborne House, Queen Victoria's villa on the Isle of Wight, built in 1845–51 by Prince Albert and Thomas Cubitt. In contrast to earlier houses in

105. Italianate: Shrubland Hall, Suffolk. Remodelled by Sir Charles Barry, 1848–54

▲ 106. Tudor-Gothic: Toddington Manor, Gloucestershire, 1819–35, by Charles Hanbury-Tracy

the classical manner, it is used with greater asymmetry of elevation, often with a campanile-like tower as the chief accent. Windows are round-arched and often linked in pairs or threes. Roofs are usually low-pitched with eaves carried on long brackets. It was as popular for some large country houses (especially those by Sir Charles Barry, e.g. Shrubland Park, Suffolk; Cliveden, Bucks.; and Trentham Hall, Staffs. (dem.)) as for more modest detached and semi-detached villas for businessmen, and even quite modest terraces. It is also the pre-eminent style among the swathe of grand terraced houses being built in the West End of London in areas like Pimlico, Belgravia, Bayswater and Kensington and in the early Victorian developments at Brighton (Kemp Town) and Bristol (Royal Promenade, Victoria Square, Clifton, c. 1851).

The Romantic aspect of the GOTHIC of the late C18 continued to inform the appearance of houses in the early C19, when there was a preoccupation with favouring national styles over 'foreign' classicism. The Gothic takes various forms over the decades from c. 1830–80 and was remarkably versatile in satisfying the self-image of occupants from the duke to the dustman. In the early Victorian

107. Gothic Revival: Scarisbrick Hall, Lancashire by Thomas Rickman, 1813–15, A.W.N. Pugin, c. 1837–45 and E.W. Pugin, 1860s

period, continuing from the late Regency, the preferred mode was TUDOR-GOTHIC, characterized by mullioned windows with four-centred arches and hoodmoulds running along the top and partly down the sides of windows. It was especially favoured among smaller houses and villas, assisted by numerous publications such as J. C. Loudon's *Encyclopedia of Cottage, Farm and Villa Architecture and Furniture* (1833), which offered Gothic as one of a number of stylistic options to builders of middle-class residences. But it also resulted in some rarer designs of ambition for country house such as Toddington Manor, Gloucestershire, of 1819–35. At the grander end of the scale it resulted in a continuation of the CASTLE STYLE of the late C18 but done with a new seriousness and ambition.

The Tudor Gothic style evolved into a revival of ELIZABETHAN and JACOBEAN styles (sometimes lumped together as 'Tudorbethan' or 'Jacobethan'), drawing on the great houses of the C16 and C17 as ideal models and understandably well suited to the large Victorian country house e.g. Crewe Hall, Cheshire. Houses in the Gothic and Tudor styles were held up to ridicule by A.W. N. Pugin in his 'True Principles' (1841), a manifesto for the GOTHIC REVIVAL of the mid-C19. This was not only concerned with a scrupulous imitation of medieval forms (of which Toddington, fig. 106, was an early exemplar) but also to recover the moral principles underlying the idea of the house as the centre of community and hospitality. In his design for Scarisbrick Hall, Lancashire, Pugin, in remodelling a Tudor-Gothic house by Thomas Rickman (1813–16), attempted to apply the same principles that he advocated for the reform of church architecture to house design, with authentic Gothic detail and, most importantly, a traditional open great hall with a screen at the heart of the plan. Whereas in the earlier period architects and their clients had been happy to apply a veneer of Gothic decoration to an existing house – literally so when the ornament was created in stucco – the new Gothic houses of the mid C19 were keen to demonstrate their moral seriousness and 'honesty' in materials and layout. In simple terms this meant houses of asymmetrical appearance, with massive walls, pointed windows, tracery or mullioned windows, tall roofs with tile or iron crestings, gables and turrets with little sense of the picturesque. A novelty is the use of polychromy, or different col-

▲ 108. No. 12 Ampton Road, Edgbaston, Birmingham, by J.H. Chamberlain, 1855. An example of the impact of High Victorian Gothic and the use of polychromy for a suburban villa

ours of stone or brick – red, yellow, blue, black – to make patterns around window arches or diaper patterns on the walls. The sources for motifs begin, as in churches, with a preference for the window shapes and ornament of the C13 and C14 but move by the mid 1860s towards a wider frame of reference including French, Venetian and others modes of Continental medieval architecture, leading to a more powerful, even severe appearance. Among smaller houses Gothic Revival was more likely to be the style applied to vicarages attached to new churches. For the average middle-class home the style is reduced to a few occasional motifs e.g. a pointed window, brick patterns, Gothic capitals of stucco foliage.

The ARTS AND CRAFTS MOVEMENT is an important offshoot of the later Gothic Revival. Not so much a style as an approach to design, it followed the principles of Pugin and John Ruskin in seeking to apply truth to materials, high standards of craftsmanship, and

an integration of decorative and fine arts, architecture included. Its representative figure is the writer and designer William Morris (1834–96) and the quintessential expression of the movement's effect on house design is the Red House, Bexleyheath (1859). Then in the country outside London, it was designed for Morris by Philip Webb in an early instance of architect and artist working together, and one in which the interior is as important as the exterior.

The Red House shows continuity with the Gothic Revival in its motifs, and again is a house with a great hall as a central element of its plan. However, its descendants among the simpler, informal and compact houses of the following decades develop from a VER-NACULAR REVIVAL in which priority is given to adherence to the traditions of local styles, materials and construction of building before 1700, to give the impression of an accretive building history, in some ways a continuation of the Picturesque tradition of the late C18 and early C19. For about the first time, such houses no longer looked to the country house for their style but to manor houses and farmhouses of the C16 and C17.

A related sub-genre of this revival has come to be called OLD ENGLISH, a style used from *c*. 1860, in which tile-hanging, tall chimneys, half-timbering and other details of the gabled vernacular domestic architecture of late medieval south-east England are picturesquely combined. The style is particularly associated with the architects George Devey, W. E Nesfield and Richard Norman Shaw, of whom the latter exploited the style to sometimes quite dramatic effect e.g. at Cragside, Northumberland, 1870–5. But most of the Arts and Crafts houses are small, low, and asymmetrical, their form largely dictated by the practical, functional arrangement of the rooms within, and designed in the round, so that all elevations have an equal importance in expressing the interior functions. Hospitality and intimacy were emphasized by large inglenook fireplaces and window seats. As there was no prescribed set of rules, architects such as Charles Voysey and Edwin Lutyens were free to evolve a variety of responses to these essential principles with houses of extremely varied appearance, determined by local

▲ 110. Old English: Hampton-in-Arden, Warwickshire. Cottages, by W. Eden Nesfield, 1868

building traditions and materials. Among the late C19 practition-
ers in this tradition much emphasis was laid on economy of planning and construction. It recommended itself strongly to houses for
occasional use, such as weekend or holiday villas for businessmen
where the full range of services were not required. While the majority of such houses were designed for individual clients, rather than
as speculative developments, it was this economical but comfortable
emphasis in Arts and Crafts houses which recommended it to the
first builders of mass housing from c. 1900.

Shaw introduced another fresh approach to house design in the
1870s with the so-called QUEEN ANNE style. This is not to be con-
fused with the architecture of the reign of Queen Anne (1702–14).
Instead it refers to a style that sought to turn away from the Gothic
Revival and evoke the domestic classical manner of mid C17 in
England. The 'Queen Anne' is best represented in Shaw's designs
for the middle-class suburb of Bedford Park in West London,
laid out in 1875. It favoured red brick or terracotta, usually combined with rubbed brick, white-painted woodwork, and Dutch or
shaped gables. The placing and shape of windows is related more
closely to the arrangements of the rooms inside and varies from
tall thin openings to generous oriels, asymmetrically placed. One
of the most identifiable motifs of the style is the so-called Ipswich
window, derived from the C17 Ancient House at Ipswich, Suffolk,
which Shaw used on Swan House, Chelsea Embankment, London.
Chimneys are tall, with bricks laid to form vertical ribs to the shafts.
A widespread motif is the sunflower, often in the form of moulded
terracotta panel or plaster pargetting (moulded or incised plaster
decoration) set into the façade. Variety is an over-riding concern,
so that even in developments of terraced housing (famously on the
Cadogan Estate, Chelsea, or Collingham Gardens, Kensington, both
designed by Ernest George & Peto in the 1880s) there is a deliberate
avoidance of consistency in elevation from house to house. These
developments were inspired in their elevations by the tradition of
tall brick building in the towns and cities of Holland and Flanders
of the Flemish Renaissance, with large frontal gables of stepped and
shaped profiles.

III. Queen Anne: Bedford Park, London. Terraced houses in the style and materials evocative of the character of late C17 and early C18 English architecture

Also overlapping with the Arts and Crafts and Queen Anne houses is the late-c19 AESTHETIC MOVEMENT, an approach to design that rejected the moral fervour behind the Gothic Revival in favour of 'art for art's sake'. The results were often eclectic, drawing typically on Renaissance, Oriental, especially Japanese, and ancient Greek sources. Seen at its strongest in interiors and furniture, the approach is most closely associated with the work of E. W. Godwin.

Alongside, but primarily restricted to the wealthiest sections of society, was a French Revival. Over the course of the second half of the c19 this takes a variety of forms. An early example is Wrest Park, Bedfordshire, designed by the amateur architect Lord de Grey in the 1830s for himself, and derived from c17 French architectural books. In the mid c19 a renewed interest in French Gothic churches and an admiration for Parisian buildings of the Second Empire under Louis-Napoleon could similarly use French late medieval and c16

▲ 112. French Revival: Wrest Park, view of s front and gardens, by Thomas Philip 2nd Earl de Grey, 1834–6

chateaux as a source for new houses with steep mansard or pavil-ion roofs with dormers. Among the most elaborate representative of this style is Waddesdon Manor, Buckinghamshire (1877–83 by H. Destailleur) and Barnard Castle, County Durham, evoking the styles of France under kings Louis XIV (1643–1715; Baroque); Louis XV (1715–74; Rococo) and Louis XVI (1774–92; Neoclassical). A market grew up in the late c19 for importing panelling and other fittings removed from French houses. Decorators and craftsmen became highly skilled in reproducing French and English c18 styles (e.g. at Luton Hoo, Beds.). Georgian houses in Mayfair, London, were often refitted in the late C19 and early C20 with whole interiors in a mixture of these styles, sometimes making it hard to distinguish between authentic and reproduction work.

The revival of interest in C17 English architecture in the Queen Anne style and in native vernacular traditions in the Arts and Crafts movement was, perhaps inevitably, followed by a renewed interest in domestic classical architecture of the end of the C17 and the beginning of the C18. Neo-William-and-Mary and NEO-GEORGIAN houses return to symmetry of façades, brick walls in Flemish bond, hipped roofs with dormers and pedimented doorcases.

House types

From the beginning of Victoria's reign until the last thirty years of the century, when agricultural depression set in, great wealth remained concentrated in the landed estates, and the ultimate expression of social position at the head of society remained the country house set in a park or large grounds. Many houses were rebuilt during this period by existing landowners, or built afresh as an emblem of success by the newly monied, who had made their fortunes in industry and commerce at home and across the Empire. In many cases the fortunes of the *nouveau riche* were instrumental in propping up the established aristocracy through judicious marriages (including, by the Edwardian period, the considerable wealth available from American heiresses).

As the C19 developed the country house evolved more and more into a place for entertaining and field sport, something which had begun in the late C18 and early C19, but which reached its summit in the period *c.* 1850–80. The planning of the country house now had to develop to cope with its multiple functions and especially the careful demarcation of spaces on hierarchical lines. This meant not only separating family from their servants but also family from guests, and separating the different grades and genders of servants from each other at mealtimes and for sleeping. Such separation was the continuation of a trend already identifiable by the early C19 when country houses began to dispense with the notion of a *piano nobile* and settled into a typical sequence on the ground floor of drawing room, library and dining room, with rooms for family activities reserved to another part. The Victorian house multiplied the number of rooms with their own functions and for use at different times of day, from breakfast rooms and morning rooms to smoking rooms and rooms for music and games, notably billiards.

Such careful planning became the specialism of a small number of architects, notably William Burn. Inside, there was greater emphasis on separating adults from children, whose nursery and schoolroom would be closer to the servants' quarters, and even husbands from wives, with the 'masculine' world of the business room, study, library, smoking room and billiard room separate from the 'feminine' morning room, drawing room and boudoir. Over the course of the century and especially in Edwardian houses the notion of the baronial hall was remade into the living hall, a curious hybrid of entrance hall and drawing room.

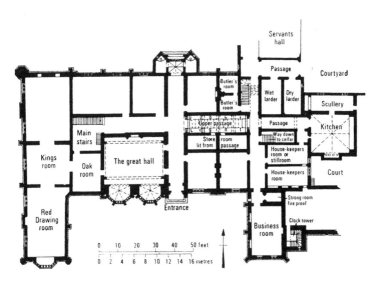

△ 114. Scarisbrick Hall, Lancashire, plan. An example of the increasingly specialised country house plan with almost half of it given over to the functions of the service wing

Access to bedrooms on the upper floor was carefully organized to avoid rooms communicating from one to another (the *enfilade* arrangement of the C17 and C18 country house). Corridors become the norm, with rooms opening off them, increasing privacy for the owners and allowing servants to pass around the house largely unseen. The earlier pattern of kitchens in pavilion wings, with the disadvantage of placing food at a considerable distance from dining rooms, was done away with in favour of kitchen and service wings directly attached to the main body of the house: these incorporated all the needs of the household and its staff, with rooms for cooking, washing, storage of food, storage of wine, and accommodation of senior staff. Externally, the result was the era of the sprawling country house, with much of the bulk accounted for by the service wing alone.

A sub-set of the Victorian country house is the house in the country, without the burden of a large estate and its management. Towards the end of the C19 many of this class of smaller house were being built in rural areas either as homes for businessmen who could reach their place of work by the expanding railway network or as weekend or holiday retreats at a safe distance from the polluted and unhealthy city centres. The Home Counties and the edges of the largest towns are one focus of this change, with extensive building of detached homes in private grounds, and others are the areas of England famed for their natural beauty, like the Lake District.

Such houses required much less servicing than major country houses and their planning is accordingly less expansive and intimate, typically reduced to a core of entrance hall (which might double as a living hall), drawing room, dining room and kitchen wing. Rooms were designed to face south to catch the best sunlight and air, seen as essential to the promotion of health, and to maximise this butterfly plans, with wings set at an angle from the central range, also became popular. Many looked for their architectural inspiration to the local vernacular (e.g. white-washed walls and slate roofs in the Lakes; red brick, tile-hanging and timber-framing in the south-east).

The country house was regarded socially as the most important type of house, but it was of course the preserve of a tiny minority.

▲ 115. Bowness-on-Windermere, Moor Cragg, by C.F.A. Voysey, 1899–1900

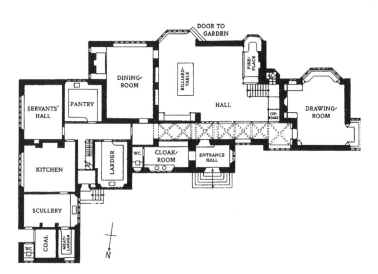

▲ 116. Bowness-on-Windermere, Blackwell, ground-floor plan

The TERRACED HOUSE and the SEMI-DETACHED HOUSE that had spread across towns in the late C18 and early C19 now burgeoned in vast numbers across the rapidly expanding urban areas to meet the demands of a growing middle class. The majority of new urban housing in the Victorian period was in the hands of speculative developers. As in the C18, owners of the land on which smarter developments were built could impose strict standards through conditions in the building leases as in London's Belgravia and Kensington. Building societies (established in 1842) could also control the quality of building through conditions attached to the loans they offered builders.

By the mid- to late Victorian period the largest terraced houses remain broadly similar to their Late Georgian predecessors but might be as high as five or even six storeys. BASEMENTS for servants and kitchens were still an essential feature but kitchens were pushed to the rear of the plan and given separate sculleries for washing. Inside, the entrance still opens to a hall passage to the stair, but the principal rooms on the ground and first floors might now include a study in addition to drawing room and dining room, and more attention was given to ensuring fine views over gardens. MEWS at the rear for stabling and carriages are also increasingly common.

Medium-size terraced houses in the mid-Victorian period were broadly similar but no more than two storeys high with basement and attic and externally simpler. Such houses dispensed with a basement (replaced by a cellar in some cases) after *c.* 1875 and instead had a longer rear wing. This gives such houses their recognizable L-plan, with two rooms and the staircase hall in the front part, and kitchen or back parlour and sculleries etc. at the rear. From this time each terrace house is typically arranged as a mirror image of its neighbour, with the doors paired and therefore entrance halls and staircases in parallel and the rear wings adjoining, an economical means for building chimney flues in the party wall. The principal deficiency was that the back room in the main body of the house was now rather ill-lit and overshadowed by the rear wing. In the small terraced house, the entrance from the street is directly into the front room rather than a hall.

117. Examples of suburban London terraces of the 1860s (top), and 1900 (bottom)

In the more well-to-do suburban developments that followed the pattern set by the houses in Bedford Park, London, broader plots made it possible to give a more square plan to the house, whether detached, semi-detached or terraced, and eliminate the rear wing. At the same time the breadth gave more room for the entrance hall without diminishing the size of the principal ground-floor rooms. Improvements in piped water supplies by the late Victorian era also made it possible to incorporate flushing lavatories and bathrooms on bedroom floors in large and medium-size houses. By 1900 the rear wing of the standard L-plan terraced house was usually two-storey to provide space for these features, as well as an extra bedroom.

The elevations of terraced houses also change. porches (full in larger houses, shallow or recessed in medium-sized houses) are added to the front door, in which stucco doorcases are commonly a hybrid type with segment-headed arches, Gothic capitals and naturalistic foliage. Flat frontages are broken from the mid- to late Victorian period by BAY WINDOWS – to the ground-floor window only in smaller houses, two-storey in larger ones – of canted form in the mid-Victorian period and by 1900 also of square form. SASH WINDOWS remain the standard form in the C19 but the availability of large sheets of cast plate glass from *c*. 1850 meant that the grid pattern of glazing bars still prevalent in the early Victorian period disappeared; most windows employed two-by-two patterns or had a single panel top and bottom. Late C19 houses designed in the 'Queen Anne' style (*see* p. 142) however returned for reasons of historical continuity to the use of small panes in the upper sashes. With the Arts and Crafts phase (*see* p. 139) and its revival of the pre-1700 vernacular styles the leaded casement window is revived, but the sash window returns in the Neo-Georgian houses of the period after 1900. Parapets, common to terraced houses of the early Victorian period, give way to exposed eaves and sometimes to GABLES animating the roofline along with hipped and half-hipped roofs, chimneys, turrets, etc. The dominance of stucco and render up to and through the Italianate phase was superseded by a preference for brick and tile instead of slates. Both materials offered opportunities for colour, ornament and pattern-making in façades, whether using contrasting brick colours, moulded bricks, or tile-hanging and tile-cresting for the roof ridge. The Queen Anne phase confirmed a preference for red brick, and the Old English for half-timbering, especially in the gables over bay windows.

Workers' and model housing

The quality of working-class housing in many of the expanding industrial areas of early C19 England was very poor and overcrowded. People attracted into the towns for work occupied a mix of old properties and newly built cheap housing of frequently bad construction, served by rudimentary drainage systems. Among new housing some distinctive types emerged, such as houses designed for a mix of residential and industrial purpose. Weavers' housing is one of the most easily identified types that would have been found in parts of East London in the C18 and C19 and also in Manchester, Leeds and other textile areas, notably the Pennine villages.

118. Paradise Street, Macclesfield, Cheshire. Early C19 houses purpose-built for weavers and superficially similar to many late Georgian terraces except for the distinctive long windows lighting the attic workrooms

A very widespread urban type to appear from the early C19 was the BACK-TO-BACK HOUSE. This was prevalent in the northern cities, where narrow plots of land were available for building: a speculative builder could profitably develop two houses, each one room deep, against each other, rather than one house with a front and back room. Terrace houses of this type were built with the door opening off the street into the ground-floor room; stairs at the back rose against the windowless common rear wall. In larger examples of this type there might be space in the attic for working use, activity strictly forbidden by landlords of middle-class houses. Such housing had the rear houses facing into long courts which had shared water, privies, etc. for communal use, and which were open at one end for removal of waste by dustmen. Access to these courts from the houses facing the street was typically through a tunnel. Some of the worst sort of urban housing gave access to the rear courts only through the house itself, creating problems of disease in the most overcrowded districts, where cholera outbreaks, caused by infected water supplies, were a major health problem. The 1848 Public Health Act improved matters by setting minimum street widths and allowing higher standards to be enforced for access to back yards for rubbish disposal etc., but proper drainage systems would be required to

▲ 119. Prince Consort Cottages, Windsor, Berkshire, 1852 by Henry Roberts. These cottages are typical of their time and show the interest taken in model housing by Prince Albert. In 1851, as part of the Great Exhibition, he commissioned Henry Roberts to design a model form of cottage (in fact four flats within a two-storey building) which could be reproduced to make a long terrace or alternatively arranged vertically as a block of flats

finally deal with the problems caused by open sewers and contaminated water.

In some parts of the country the largest industrial enterprises could afford to develop housing for their skilled workers along model lines. Saltaire, in the West Riding of Yorkshire, laid out in 1850–3 by Titus Salt, is among the first large-scale model villages, with rows of terraces, semi-detached and detached houses for the employees in his woollen mills, as well as a full range of amenities for their spiritual, educational and health needs.

The movement for housing reform began *c.* 1840 and emphasized the provision of adequate accommodation for working people to counter the effects of rapidly increasing populations in the major cities. The lead was taken by philanthropic bodies such as the Society for Improving the Condition of the Labouring Classes (founded in 1844), which developed standard plans for simple cottages and flats that could be executed by a builder. The lessons of this were taken up by some of the larger landowners for the design of estate cottages.

In the more congested urban areas, it was necessary to build high because of the value of land, even in slum districts, and from about 1860 new forms of large blocks of model TENEMENTS appeared in several of the major English cities. London led the way. Much of this was due to philanthropic organizations, principally the Peabody Trust (founded in 1862), which erected 'estates' of large four-storey blocks set around a courtyard. Early Victorian model flats, or tenements, are typically blocks of up to five storeys, with access to the individual dwellings provided by an open staircase rising to gallery-type iron balconies running along the front.

▲ 120. Turner Court, Hull, Yorkshire. This block of model housing, built in 1862, was constructed by the Society for Improving the Condition of the Labouring Classes. It was their only housing project outside London

▲   121. Boundary Estate, Bethnal Green, East London. A very early example
of large blocks of flats by the architects of the London County Council's
Housing Branch. They were much influenced by the ideals of William Morris
and the architecture of Philip Webb and Norman Shaw. Note for example
the use of different colours of brick to achieve patterns in the façades without expense

▶   122. This section drawing shows the layout of a type of terraced housing
built in Tyneside (primarily found in Newcastle, Gateshead and Sunderland).
Externally it looks like a typical small Victorian terraced house, but there
are two doors to the street, one leading to the ground-floor flat, and the
other opening directly to the staircase to the upper flat, which had further
accommodation in the attic. 'Cottage flats' related to this type of housing
are found elsewhere in late C19 and early C20 working-class suburbs

Later in the C19 building companies were established, usually on a philanthropic model, but they also attempted to attract private investors for their schemes in the expectation of a modest return. In 1890 the Housing of the Working Classes Act made it possible for the elected local authorities to clear areas and build new housing themselves. While London's new County Council acted on this, it was the exception: the majority of councils in the cities were content to leave house building to the private sector.

In all the model housing schemes there was an unresolved difference between those reformers who believed that shared entrance staircases should be left open to the street for ventilation and that no flat should have its own WC and those who believed in the need for tenants to have private facilities in their flats. Something agreed on by all was that adolescent boys and girls should have separate bedrooms, hitherto the privilege only of wealthy families.

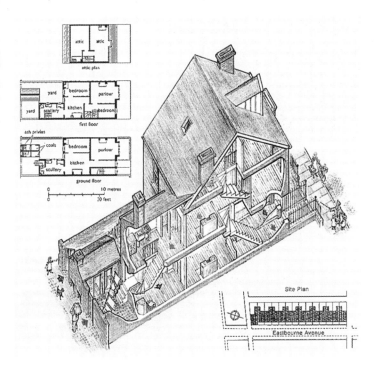

▲ 123. Port Sunlight, Cheshire, provided by Lord Leverhulme for workers at
his soap factory is architecturally the most distinguished model village for
workers. It was mostly built between 1888 and 1910 and consciously emulated the spacious, leafy setting and picturesque variety of houses in the
best middle-class suburbs

Legislation was introduced in many towns in the 1860s and
1870s to regulate standards of sanitation and building. It was
not always very effective, but gradually prohibited the building
of back-to-back housing and other unsanitary types of domestic building. Private speculative builders still provided the vast
majority of new housing in the cities where standards were poor-
est, but many evolved their own forms of model dwelling suited
to local demands.

Later in the C19, in response to the increasingly unattractive conditions of inner cities, the concept of the GARDEN CITY emerged.
It came from Ebenezer Howard's book *Tomorrow: The Peaceful*

Path to Real Reform (1898; republished in 1902 as *Garden Cities of Tomorrow*), which envisaged a town designed from scratch as an independent and self-sufficient unit, and striking a careful balance in the social mix and size of the population, types of housing and types of industry. The first Garden City was Letchworth, Hertfordshire, begun in 1903 with Raymond Parker and Barry Unwin as architects, and strongly rooted in the principles of the Arts and Crafts movement. Related to this idea but without the dependence on being economically self-sufficient is the GARDEN SUBURB – most famously developed at Hampstead, North London, begun in 1907 – conceived as an ideal layout of houses with gardens and with the intention, in contrast to most suburbs, of making houses for a range of social levels.

The principles of the Garden City were also echoed in the latest generation of model villages set out by industrialists such as Lord Leverhulme at Port Sunlight in Cheshire, the Cadbury family at Bournville in Birmingham, Joseph Rowntreee at New Earswick in York (1904), and Joseph Reckitt's factory workers' housing in Hull (1907–8) as well as the more enlightened mining companies in the Yorkshire and Derbyshire coalfields. These settlements showcase the varied revival styles of the Old English and Arts and Crafts version of Tudor, often with frontal gables at the centre of the façade and a single living room inside running from front to back. There were detached, semi-detached and terraced houses of varied 'classes' in these settlements, but even the cheapest class demonstrates advances in planning – all the houses included baths (upstairs in the best houses; in the scullery for cheaper ones). After the interval of the First World War (during which some new garden villages were set out for workers engaged in arms production) the houses of the garden cities, suburbs and villages proved a decisive influence on the new public housing built by the councils.

6 THE TWENTIETH CENTURY TO THE PRESENT

The First World War and the two decades following it brought about a transformation in housing as a political and social issue, while also heralding the end of the country house and its estate. Housing was one of the central issues for Liberal Prime Minister Lloyd George's election campaign in 1918. Central government passed a series of housing acts beginning with the so-called Addison Act in 1919, which marks the beginning of the tradition of state-provided housing. At that time the supply of mass housing at subsidized rents was the responsibility of the Ministry of Health, continuing from the late Victorian and Edwardian preoccupation with clearing congested slums and building model housing for fewer inhabitants as essential to good health. During the war sub-standard homes were blamed for having produced men unfit for military service, and it was feared that a return to the slums for many might foment revolution. For the first time subsidies were granted to local authorities, spreading the cost of housing between government, local ratepayers and the tenants themselves. The aim was to build half a million new 'homes for heroes', to answer a chronic shortage that the private builders were regarded as being unable to fulfil. Progress was slow and required encouragement from subsequent housing acts by the first Labour government in 1923 and 1924. There is an ebb and flow over the course of the interwar years between setting out new estates in suburban or extra-urban locations (what would now be called 'greenfield sites') to meet the housing shortage, largely the pattern before the onset of the Depression in 1929. The Housing Act of 1930 changed subsidies in favour of building high-density flats in slum clearance areas.

Interwar housing

The theories of planning and design of much new state-subsidized housing derived directly from the Garden City movement through

124. Manor Estate, Sheffield. Aerial view. A good example of a 'cottage estate' with streets set out in radial patterns of circles and half-circles, and low-density housing of semi-detached and terraced cottages

the involvement of Raymond Unwin, the architect of Letchworth, as a member of the Tudor Walters Committee that reported on post-war reconstruction. The committee set down standards for design and layout of housing as a guide for local authorities. As a consequence the majority of the new housing of this period, regardless of its location, is typified by the 'COTTAGE ESTATE', which follows the Garden City and garden suburb principles of low-density developments (typically just twelve houses per acre): semi-detached cottages (or four-in-ones) with front and back gardens, cultivation of which was an important expectation of tenants, encouraged by annual competitions. The style of these cottages is a version of the

Arts and Crafts revival of English vernacular, with roughcast walls and gables, or Neo-Georgian, but treated with economy so that there is very little enrichment of details. The other similarity with the garden suburbs was a policy of placing houses at angles to create a more picturesque setting, and especially the avoidance of monotonous straight streets in favour of geometric layouts of streets in crescents, circles and semicircles. It is this form of planning that makes such estates easy to recognize on a map or from the air. Among the largest and most famous are the Becontree Estate, at Dagenham in East London (London County Council Architects, 1919–35), and Wythenshawe in Manchester (begun in 1931 by Barry Parker).

Although some efforts were made to create socially mixed estates (and the rents of much early post-war council housing were far from cheap, thereby giving preference to better-off skilled workers), the visual variety aimed at in the original garden suburbs and garden cities was usually sacrificed in favour of a few stock designs that were endlessly repeated and resulted in a monotony of appearance. Some early inhabitants of large housing schemes complained of an inability to distinguish their street from any other. The houses themselves varied in type from two- to four-bedroom dwellings and with a varying degree of separation between the rooms, so that a great many for the first time extended the middle-class norm of one living room (for general family use) and one parlour (for special occasions) to working-class families. A major change is the adoption of wider fronts for houses (to avoid the narrow type of terrace house with long rear projections) and more generous standards of space within.

Local authority housing could only meet a proportion of the need after 1918 and much more familiar is the private, speculatively built suburban house. London alone doubled in area after 1918 and about 860,000 new houses were built before 1939. The local authority contribution amounted to not much more than one-fifth, and a similar pattern can be traced in other large cities. The size of the middle class greatly increased in the early C20, but people were less well-off than before, and the interwar private house is somewhat smaller than its C19 predecessor, with room for domestic help but not servants.

▲ 125. Miall Road, Hall Green, Birmingham, by H. Dare & Co., 1936. Textbook examples of the semi-detached houses built by private builder–developers across interwar England

Encouraged by the railway network small and larger firms of builders and building societies (which expanded greatly in the 1920s to offer mortgages to a much wider range of people) erected 'mock-Tudor' houses in expanding suburbs. These have come to be seen as the epitome of the interwar house. They are the descendants of the 'Old English' houses of Norman Shaw and others reduced to a few repetitive motifs, conveying an image of rural nostalgia. A cliché of the kind is a two-storey bow or canted bay on the front, usually with a half-timbered gable over, with the door in a porch or recessed behind a brick or tile arch; the walls are of brick with pebbledash, render, tile-hanging or half-timbering, and there is stained glass for the front doors and staircase landing windows – small but important distinctions from contemporary council housing. Front gardens are the norm, and at the more expensive end of development much attention is sometimes given to the wider environment in the form of tree-planting and grass verges separating the pavements from the road. Inside, improvements to the supply of services – water, gas and electricity – made homes more comfortable and increased public interest in the style and planning of interiors (the annual 'Ideal Home' Exhibition was launched by the *Daily Mail* in 1908). Greater importance was placed on the style and fittings of bathrooms and kitchens, which became the domain of the housewife rather than a domestic servant. Some of the largest building firms of the present day (e.g. Wimpey and Laing) were developed from this time, from roots set down in the C19.

Garages, for the new motor cars, became more widespread very gradually from the 1920s onwards (their modest dimensions unsuitable for C21 cars), tucked into the space at the side or just behind the house and later integrated into the design of the house itself in the more expensive houses. Garages associated with council housing before the Second World War are unusual, as car ownership was uncommon even among skilled workers. It is for this reason that so many interwar houses on council cottage estates and the cheaper

▲ 126. No. 78, Derngate, Northampton, by C.R. Mackintosh, 1916. A startling decorative scheme for a terraced house of its date anticipating the angular motifs of the Art Deco style of the 1920s

▲ 127. Barford Court, Kingsway, Hove, 1934–7, by Robert Cromie, better known as a cinema architect. Detail of the staircase

end of private suburban developments have had to sacrifice their front gardens to parking space, where narrow streets leave little room for cars.

So popular was the typical 1920s and 1930s style of suburban house that it is rare to find speculatively built homes in the suburbs daring to venture fully into the bold shapes of the then fashionable ART DECO style. It does occur from time to time, however, in developments of serviced flats, a feature of the higher-toned London suburbs, where an enthusiasm is also displayed for neocolonial styles, such as Cape Dutch, derived from the white walls and Dutch gables of South Africa, or Spanish haciendas with pantile roofs, sometimes glazed blue or green.

▲ 128. Great House, Dedham, Essex by Raymond Erith, 1937–8, strongly reminiscent of the work of Sir John Soane

Builders created these suburban houses without the cost of employing architects, whose involvement in interwar housing is confined primarily to larger detached houses in the more fashionable suburbs or to the most expensive kind of house built in the commuter towns and villages around London. Closer to the First World War such houses are more likely to be a continuation of the Arts and Crafts tradition running concurrently with Neo-Georgian. Among the architects pursuing a scholarly revival of the domestic CLASSICISM of the late C18 and early C19 were Albert Richardson and Raymond Erith and several other architects and interior designers in this period found no contradiction between the austerity of Late Georgian and Regency houses and the unornamented styles of architecture emerging from the continent in the 1920s and 30s. Houses responding to the new architectural ideas that gained currency around 1930 in a fully developed MODERNIST style are unheard of in local authority work (except in flats – *see* below), and exceptionally rare in speculative developments, where they seem to be restricted to builder-developers prepared to take a risk on finding purchasers for houses with plain walls, cubic massing and flat roofs. Instead such innovations are primarily reserved for the one-off private commissions from architects drawing on the latest ideas from the Continent, strengthened by the presence in England of émigré architects from Europe. In spite of appearances, many 'modern' houses in the 1930s were still built according to traditional methods. Apparently of concrete, these turn out on close inspection to be no more than brick structures with a skin of coloured render – hardly

▲ 129. Concrete House, Westbury-on-Trym, Bristol, by Amyas Connell, 1934. An especially well-preserved example of a Modernist house of the 1930s and one consiously adopting a new material to advertise its modernity. The house has a thin concrete frame infilled with concrete blocks, thin cornices shading the windows, a recessed balcony with columns or pilotis and bands of steel-framed windows. The railing around the flat roof indicates its use as a roof terrace

▲ 130. St Andrew's Gardens, Liverpool, completed 1935. Flats built by the City
Council (Director of Housing, Lancelot Keay; design by his assistant John
Hughes). The main element is a five-storey, D-shaped block (the model was
Bruno Taut and Martin Wagner's Horseshoe Estate, Berlin, admired by Keay
on a visit in 1931) with continuous balconies overlooking a central court

different from the practice of speculative builders of the early C19 of
covering terraced houses in stucco to emulate stone.

However, concrete- or steel-framed construction with brick facing was being used by this time for multi-storey blocks of flats. A
type of housing to which there was much resistance in the C19, flats
become a much more common feature of housing between the wars,
especially in cities like London, Liverpool and Manchester. Local
authority flats constructed in slum clearance areas in the 1920s and
1930s were built much higher than before but were still limited in
their number of storeys by, on the one hand, building regulations
that prescribed heights in relation to width of streets, and on the
other, the fact that flats of this type had no lifts and therefore access
to all floors was by stair. It was also necessary to ensure that the

top floors were within reach of a fireman's ladder. Typically inter-war flats are therefore no more than four or five storeys high, with a horizontal layout, a stair tower serving all floors, and access to each flat by means of a balcony along the front. Access by corridor, or from a common staircase, as would have been standard in many private blocks of flats of this period, is extremely rare. Flats of this period were built at lower densities than the congested tenements of the Victorian period and are more generously planned inside. The kitchen and WC are always immediately inside the entrance, facing on to the balcony for privacy and to reduce noise inside.

Building systems of the kind introduced in France, America and Germany for construction of multi-storey flats were the preserve of a few specialist firms of engineers, and confined to major projects; Britain was notably late to adopt such innovations. The Quarry Hill estate in Leeds (begun in 1935) was the first housing to take up a

▲ 131. Quarry Hill estate, Leeds

system devised by Vladimir Bodiansky, chief engineer of the French engineers Mopin, for prefabricated concrete panels on a steel frame. Quarry Hill was unique in rising to a height of eight storeys, requiring the use of lifts for the first time in a council-built scheme.

Quarry Hill is important for another reason – it was the first public housing scheme in England consciously to aim to reproduce the type of housing developments then being promoted in Vienna, with a full range of amenities for the estate (although the scheme was never carried out). This was an ideal central to the theories promoted for mass housing by younger, progressive, architects associated with Modernism and experimented with in a few private schemes in London in the 1930s: the Isokon flats in Highgate by Wells Coates; the nearby Highpoint flats by Berthold Lubetkin and Tecton; and Kensal House, Ladbroke Grove, London, by Maxwell Fry, erected by the Gas, Light and Coke Company as a model scheme, with nursery school, social clubs, allotments and tenants' committee. The flats were also a model for the provision of fully fitted kitchens, partly as a means of demonstrating the company's own products, at a time when the tenants of many working-class flats were still expected to cook on a range in the living room.

These Modernist schemes were also among the first to make use of REINFORCED CONCRETE construction as an essential aspect of the architecture, unconcealed by brick or other facing. This was far from cheap and only a very few engineers in England, notably Ove Arup, had the technical knowledge to advise architects wishing to build in this material. A novel feature of this period in houses, also continued after the war, are PILOTIS, the French term for pillars or stilts that support a building above an open ground floor. Also central to the image of the Modernist house was the steel-framed window, the best known of which is the 'Crittall' window made in Essex, which could take the form of a traditional casement or a horizontal band of windows wrapped around a corner for smooth effect.

This concentration on the medium and smaller houses and flats built by councils and private developers for the vast majority of the population indicates the wider truth of the decline of the country house in the first half of the c20. The combined effect of agricultural depression, taxation, death duties, and the First World War depriv-

132. Plumpton Place, East Sussex, by Edwin Lutyens, 1933–5; one of his last houses in the Surrey vernacular of his youth but also typical of the period for its revival of the style of C16 and C17 houses

ing country houses of heirs brought a halt to new building, a reduction in the extent of estates and their sale. As noted earlier, there had already been a clear trend in new country houses of the late C19 and in the years preceding the First World War towards the 'house in the country' – a large and impressive house for entertaining funded increasingly by business interests. The inter-war generation of houses was developed to a more compact form, often deliberately more self-effacing and informal than the bombastic High Victorian houses, and dependent on a smaller body of servants, not least as a result of the technologies available to reduce the labour involved in much housework.

An interesting trend in such houses after 1918 is the enthusiasm for returning to Tudor styles, suggestive of an historical continuity for the house and its owner. Many genuine C16 and C17 houses were being demolished at this time and it is common not only to find houses being built in an earlier style but also ones that incorporate architectural woodwork or panelling salvaged from older houses.

Housing since the Second World War

The Second World War demanded large-scale planning and technical innovation in many areas, including mass production, which architects were keen to exploit. The Dudley Committee on housing, formed in 1942, was an update of the 1919 Tudor Walters Committee; weighing heavily in the committee's mind was the failure of the 'homes for heroes' programme unleashed by its predecessor – in particular its costs and the lack of integrated thinking on the estates. Much of the committee's work was devoted to the choice of the type of dwelling – flat, semi-detached house or terraced house – and the arrangement of the family's activities within the home. The results of their investigations reflect a changing society, so that, for example, the advent of widely available gas and electricity had changed peoples' expectations, not least those of women, who had been employed in industries and lived in hostels where services were of a high standard. Many women's groups were consulted in the survey and their responses take us beyond simple questions of design. They hoped that a minimum standard of housing should be guaranteed, providing a decent and healthy setting for family life.

In 1944 the Dudley Report was published along with the government's *Housing Manual*. This encouraged lifts for all buildings over three storeys; staircases instead of balcony access; and maisonettes as well as flats – the report made it clear that flats were unsuitable as family homes. In the period 1945–7 some good housing was built to the improved standards. Central heating, better systems for refuse disposal, ventilated internal bathrooms and balconies were now expected.

Among the first types of housing to be produced in many areas were the 'prefabs' – single-storey bungalows of prefabricated (i.e. factory-made) parts that could be rapidly assembled by unskilled labour to meet temporary needs. In fact large numbers remained in occupation well into the beginning of this century. Other forms of prefabricated two-storey house were also widely used in the 1940s and early 1950s, including among others a steel-framed type made by the British Iron and Steel Federation, the prototype for which was designed by Frederick Gibberd, and the 'Cornish' house made

▲ 133. Prefabricated houses at Gosforth, Newcastle. These examples were made by Tarran Industries Ltd and provided by the government under the Housing (Temporary Accommodation) Act of 1944. Several industries turned from war production to making prefabricated parts for housing or new schools

of concrete panels using waste from Cornwall's china clay industry with concrete tile mansard roofs.

The tradition, begun in the interwar period, of large quantities of housing being provided by local authorities was gradually revived post-war to meet the demands in the cities for reconstruction. Slum clearance programmes that had been interrupted by the war resumed, often with the intention of planning entirely new neighbourhoods, separated into zones for different activities. State provision became the principal means by which much of post-war England's housing was supplied between 1945 and 1980; and for the first time much of it was to be designed by architects employed by local authorities.

▲ 134. The Lawn, Harlow, Essex, by Frederick Gibberd, 1950–1

Low-rise schemes were planned in the manner of the earlier c20 garden suburbs and cottage estates, inheriting the English tradition of separating homes from industry and giving emphasis to landscaping of the green spaces. This appealed as much to those who deplored the private and municipal suburban sprawls of the 1930s for aesthetic and social reasons as to those who desired a more rational, technical role for modern architecture. Architecturally the post-war council house looks very different from its pre-war forerunner. The most radical architects were inspired by Le Corbusier's vision of towers in parkland or the towers of flats being built in Scandinavia, where architects and designers could see examples of social democracy in politics and Modernism in architecture working together. The mantra was still for low-density housing schemes and building vertically appeared to be the answer, leaving a generous ratio of open space per person. The first tall block of flats after the war was at Harlow, Essex, one of the 'New Towns' developed outside London, but the most famous example of the new ideal is represented by the Alton Estate at Roehampton in South London, designed by the London County Council Architects Department (1952–8). This, it was argued, also followed in the c18 and early c19 Picturesque tradition of buildings in a landscaped park. But the luxury of being able to design for sites with such interesting topography was the exception rather than the rule.

The building of high flats combined the ideas of Continental Modernism with the structural innovation of engineers, especially in the development of the CROSS-WALL SYSTEM, also known as the 'egg-crate', for framing. It had been used in the Highpoint flats at Highgate, London in the 1930s (*see* p. 170). One of the earliest post-war POINT BLOCKS – a block with flats fanning out from a central core of lifts, staircases, etc. – was The Lawn, built in 1950–1 as the centrepiece of one of the neighbourhoods of the New Town at Harlow, which also featured rows of cottages, terraced houses and larger blocks of flats. This approach became known as the mixed estate, comprising high-, medium- and low-rise housing blocks. A large example is Churchill Gardens, Pimlico, London, by Powell & Moya.

▲ 135. Churchill Gardens, Pimlico, London, 1947–62 by Powell & Moya. A large example of a 'mixed estate', the high blocks take the form of long, rectangular, SLAB BLOCKS, where the flats are approached via corridors or galleries from service cores at intervals or towers at the ends

Many of the first generation of 'set-piece' housing estates of the first decade or so after the end of the war were imaginatively planned, generous in terms of space in each dwelling and with a high level of attention to detail in their planning and appearance, including the landscaping around them.

From the 1960s, however, the widespread use of industrialized building techniques was strongly encouraged by the government of the time and lobbied for by the contractors, who developed their own BUILDING SYSTEMS for the manufacture of components in factories which could be brought to a site and assembled by unskilled labour. Architects played a much-reduced role once they were limited to choosing from a small range of options. This enforced more rigid layouts, plainer detailing, and (to be more economical) larger estates and taller buildings. More and more public housing was now concentrated in TOWER BLOCKS of identical design or regimented concrete slabs – local authorities often entered into agreements with a single supplier, resulting in identical towers across an area. Such developments were made possible by the ability to drive deep piles into the ground to support the frame of the tower and the introduction of tower cranes to raise the wall components into place on the frame. More and more of this housing was used for families, a group for whom low-rise housing was originally reserved.

The collapse of Ronan Point, a block of flats in Newham, East London, following a gas explosion in 1968 heightened public dissatisfaction and mistrust of system building. By that date government policy had already turned away from subsidizing towers and was beginning to encourage refurbishment of older housing.

Alternatives to high-rise housing were explored in many cities. Lillington Gardens, Pimlico, London, of 1961–72 by Darbourne & Darke for Westminster City Council, is a notable example of build-

136. Park Hill, Sheffield, by J. L. Womersley (with Jack Lynn and Ivor Smith) 1955–61. This was one of the most serious attempts to combine high-density housing in an urban location with ingenuity of planning and the realization of 'streets in the sky', in the form of decks wide enough to drive a milk float along. Park Hill has been listed, but extensively refurbished as private housing

ing at high density (210 persons per acre) for some 2,000 people without having to resort to high-rise slabs or towers, and with all the necessary amenities for residents. The flats and maisonettes face inwards to communal gardens. The façades are animated by the rhythmic projection and recession of the balconies. The choice of brown brick, responding to the Victorian church on the site, was a novelty at a time when system building was the standard for mass housing.

▲ 137. Lillington Gardens Estate, Westminster, London, by Darbourne & Darke, 1961-72. This section shows the ingenious interior planning with split levels and 'scissor-plan' flats that cross over each other to give outlooks on two sides

◀ 138. Vale House, Jesmond, Newcastle, 1966–8, by Douglass Wise & Partners with the Newcastle City Housing Architect, a textbook example of a late 1960s tower block in a suburban area. Over twenty-five storeys high, it is of the type assembled from components made in a factory and assembled on site

Until the 1970s private developers had reduced opportunities for building housing in areas where local authorities were taking the lead, but some sought opportunities to provide more intimate scaling in their housing and a use of traditional materials within a Modernist idiom.

As disillusionment set in with the products of the public housing programmes of the 1960s, the main change to be noted in the early 1970s is the abandonment of the imagery of the Modern Movement in favour of a revival of traditional forms and materials and cottagey layouts, sometimes known as NEO-VERNACULAR. A precursor of this trend was the rural housing built in Norfolk and Suffolk villages by Tayler & Green from the late 1940s onwards and codified in 1973 for one part of the country by Essex County Council's influential *Design Guide for Residential Areas*, which not only advocated tradi-

▲ 139. New Ash Green by Eric Lyons and SPAN, 1968–9. This was one of several schemes by SPAN with low, ingenious layouts of houses and flats around courtyards or communal lawns, intended for middle-class professionals. The details easily distinguished them from council estates of this period

▲ 140. The Studio, Ulting, Essex, by Richard and Su Rogers, 1968–9, the artist Humphrey Spender

tional materials but encouraged housing that fitted into its environment. The liberation of housing from the conformities of the 1960s can be appreciated in the wide variety of designs for housing in the New Town of Milton Keynes.

At the same time the whole notion of the large council estate was being questioned. After 1980, when the 'Right to Buy' saw properties on many older council estates sold to their tenants – who often showed their independence externally by replacing the standard issue front door – and the architectural departments of most local authorities began to be reduced, many of the most imaginative kinds of new housing were in the hands of housing associations, the successors of the C19 charitable and philanthropic providers. Often working on small sites, they signalled a break with the orthodoxy of municipal housing by the style of their houses and flats and rediscovered the ability to design avowedly modern housing with a greater sense of local context. Elsewhere, local authorities in the

last twenty to thirty years have attempted to deal with problems of appearance and performance by relinquishing control to semi-independent bodies, which have reclad entire tower blocks or made selective demolitions and rebuilt. At the time of writing some of the largest estates of the 1960s in London have been or are being replaced.

Against this trend the late C20 saw something of a revival of the country house. The period after the Second World War was one of both the destruction of many country houses (estimated at as many as 1,000 in the period 1945–55) and also the reduction of their extent and remodelling as smaller houses better suited to the economies of their age; some even reverted to the Georgian core of a house before its inflation in the C19 with commodious guest and servant wings. Almost all the new country houses since 1945 fall into this category of replacement or adaptation. Many of the other examples are conservative in appearance, favouring Neo-Georgian or Neo-Regency, but others take a more radical approach of a Modernist pavilion (e.g. Witley Park, Surrey, by Patrick Gwynne, 1960–1) or something altogether more strikingly adventurous, such as the New House, Wadhurst, East Sussex by John Outram, 1978-86. This is a house that also reflects the money and confidence to build which has come back to this house type, assisted since the 1980s by some relaxations in planning law which have facilitated the building of country houses on new sites. One-off smaller private houses have also continued to provide field for innovation: one may see a direct line of descent between the C18 villa in its garden and the post-war ideal for many of the Modernist single-storey flat-roofed pavilion with glazed sides, such as The Studio, Ulting (see p. 181), of a kind often termed Miesian in reference to the crystalline boxes designed by Mies van de Rohe (1886–1969).

141. Byker Wall, Newcastle, by Ralph Erskine, 1973–80, the most significant public housing development of the 1970s, consciously turning away from the grim repetitiveness and lack of individuality in so much municipal housing of the 1960s. The snaking 'Byker Wall' screened and protected the estate from a planned motorway while also creating intimate public spaces planted with trees. The elevations of the flats themselves are a lively mix of materials, colours and shapes, giving personality back to the home

Meanwhile private developers and the large firms of house builders since the 1980s have been relied on once more for the majority of new housing. Traditional patterns – neo-vernacular, Neo-Georgian, Neo-Regency, Neo-Victorian – are now to be found rubbing along together on the edge of towns across the country, in a manner which superficially owes something to the village of Poundbury, Dorset, created as a model settlement on the edge of Dorchester from 1989

143. Jubilee Wharf, Penryn, Cornwall, by Bill Dunster of ZED factory, 2006

142. New House, Wadhurst, East Sussex, by John Outram, from 1979 onwards

by the Duchy of Cornwall. The experience in the major English cities since the 1990s has been a return to building high-rise flats once more, not at the behest of local authorities but as private ventures. A disproportionately large percentage of such developments offer small flats, with just one or two bedrooms, at a time when the greatest need is for family homes. Architectural innovation in such large schemes remains a rarity, but as the late C20 and early C21 have added to the mix houses designed for energy efficiency and sustainable use of materials and natural resources, an idea with roots in the 1960s, there have been encouraging signs. One of the most important housing developments of recent times is the BedZed development at Beddington, London, by the architect Bill Dunster, for the Peabody Trust in 2002. It combines housing, workshops and gardens. Although not, as yet, widely taken up, it was followed by a mixed-use scheme on the same carbon-neutral principles at Jubilee Wharf, Penryn, Cornwall, in 2006.

FURTHER READING

Airs, M., 1996
The Tudor and Jacobean Country House: A Building History

Airs, M. and Tyack, G. (eds), 2007
The Renaissance Villa in Britain, 1500–1700

Alcock, N.W. and Hall, L., 1994
Fixtures and Fittings in Dated Houses 1567–1763

Aslet, C., 1982
The Last Country Houses

Aslet, C. and Powers, A., 1985
The National Trust Book of the English House

Ayres, J., 2003
Domestic Interiors: the British Tradition 1500–1850

Brunskill, R.W., 3rd edn 1987
Illustrated Handbook of Vernacular Architecture

Brunskill, R.W., 1981, rev. edn 2004
Traditional Buildings of Britain: an Introduction to Vernacular Architecture and its Revival

Burnett, J., 1978
A Social History of Housing 1815–1970

Christie, C., 2000
The British Country House in the Eighteenth Century

Clifton-Taylor, A., 1972
The Pattern of English Building

Cooper, N., 1999
Houses of the Gentry, 1480–1680

Crawford, D., ed., 1975
A Decade of British Housing 1963–73

Cunnington, P., 2006
How Old Is Your House?

Daunton, M.J., 1983
House and Home in the Victorian City: Working Class Housing 1850–1914

Emery, A., 1996
Greater Medieval Houses of England and Wales 1300–1500, vol. 1
Northern England (1996); vol. 2 *Central England and Wales* (2000);
vol. 3 *Southern England* (2006)

Emery, A., 2007
Discovering Medieval Houses in England and Wales

Franklin, J., 1981
The Gentleman's Country House and its Planning 1835–1914

Girouard, M., 1971 (reprinted with corrections 1973, revised and
enlarged 1979)
The Victorian Country House

Girouard, M., 1978
Life in the English Country House; a Social and Architectural History

Glendinning, M., and Muthesius, S., 1994
*Tower Block: Modern Public Housing in England, Scotland, Wales
and Northern Ireland*

Gomme A. and Maguire, A., 2008
Design and Plan in the Country House

Gould, J., 1977
Modern Houses in Britain 1919–39

Gray, E., 1994
The British House

Hall, M., 2009
The Victorian Country House

Hitchmough, W., 2000
The Arts and Crafts Home

Howard, M., 1987
The Early Tudor Country House

Jensen, F., 2012
Modernist Semis and Terraces in England

Jeremiah, D., 2000
Architecture and Design for the Family in Britain 1900–1970

Johnson, A., 2008
Understanding the Edwardian and Inter-war House

Knight, C., 2009
London's Country Houses

Long, H., 1993
The Edwardian House

Long, H., 2001
Victorian Houses and their Details

Mercer, E., 1975
English Vernacular Houses: a Study of Traditional Farmhouses and Cottages

Muthesius, H., 1979 (ed. with an introduction by D. Sharp, trans. by J. Seligman; originally published in German, in 3 vols 1904–5)
The English House

Muthesius, S., 1982
The English Terraced House

Penoyre, J. and J., 1978
Houses in the Landscape: A Regional Study of Vernacular Building Styles in England and Wales

Platt, C., 1994
The Great Rebuildings of Tudor and Stuart England

Quiney, A., 1986
House and Home: History of the Small English House

Robinson, J.M., 1984
The Latest Country Houses

Scofield, J., 1995
Medieval London Houses

Saumarez-Smith, C., 1993
Eighteenth-Century Decoration, Design and Domestic Interior in England

Service, A., 1982
Edwardian Interiors

Summerson, J., (1953, 8th edition 1991)
Architecture in Britain

Sutcliffe, A., ed., 1974
Multi-storey Living: the British Working Class Experience

Swenarton, M., 2008
Building the New Jerusalem

Tarn, J.N., 1973

Five Per Cent Philanthropy: an Account of Housing in Urban Areas, 1840–1914

Thompson, M., 1995
The Medieval Hall: The Basis of Secular Domestic Life, 600–1600 AD

Thornton, P., 1978, reprinted with corrections 1979
Seventeenth Century Interior Decoration in England, France and Holland

Thornton, P., 1984
Authentic Decor, the Domestic Interior 1620–1920

Tinniswood, A., 2002
The Art Deco House: Avant Garde Houses of 1920s–1930s

Weston, R., 2002
The House in the Twentieth Century

Wilson, R., and Mackley, A., 2000
Creating Paradise: the Building of the English Country House 1660–1800

Wood, M.E., 1966
The English Medieval House

Yorke, T., 2008
British Architectural Styles

INDEX OF TERMS

ILLUSTRATION SOURCES AND CREDITS

A. F. Kersting: 69. Alison Maguire: 36, 53. Angelo Hornak: 1, 10, 21, 34, 39, 41, 86, 118, 119, 139. (after plans by) Anthony Emery, *Greater Medieval Houses of England and Wales*, vol. I, 1996: 5. *Architectural Review* 148, 1970: 137. Batty Langley, *Gothick Architecture Improved*, 1742: 84. Bridgeman Art Library / Victoria Art Gallery: 82. Bruce White: 76. C.H. Wood Ltd.: 131. Charles O'Brien: 99. Colen Campbell, *Vitruvius Britannicus*, 1717-25, vol. III: 72. Corbis / Stevens Fremont: 88. *Country Life*: 52, 132. © Crown copyright. Historic England Archive: 4, 28, 37, 51, 63. Eddie Ryle-Hodges: 22. Edward Roberts, *Hampshire Houses 1250-1700: Their Dating and Development*, 2003: 11. Eric Berry: 87, 143. H. Muthesius, *The English House*, translated by J. Seligman and S. Spencer, vol. 1, 2007, courtesy of Francis Lincoln Ltd.: 116. Hilary Morgan / Alamy Stock Photo: 60. © Historic England Archive: 8, 13, 17, 18, 19, 29, 42, 47, 55, 56, 58, 61, 65, 68, 70, 71, 75, 77, 78, 80, 81, 83, 89, 92, 93, 94, 96, 100, 101, 102, 103, 106, 107, 108, 115, 120, 121, 122, 125, 127, 128, 129, 130, 133, 136, 138, 140, 141. By permission of Historic England Archive: 40, 48, 64, 66, 90, 123, 134, 135. James Austin: 59, 67. James O. Davies: 30, 35. Jeremy Milln: 26. John Britton, *Descriptive Sketches of Tunbridge Wells and the Calverley Estate*, 1832: 95. John Harris, *The Palladian Revival: Lord Burlington, His Villa and Garden at Chiswick*, 1994: 73 . John Outram: 142. John Roan: 24, 43, 54, 62, 110, 112, 126. Marquess of Tavistock and the Trustees of the Bedford Estates: 79. Mark Girouard, *The Victorian Country House*, 1979: 114. Martin Charles: 33, 97, 111. Maurice Howard: 31. National Trust Images: 3, 91; (Andreas von Einsiedel): 46. National Trust Photo Library: 25, 45, 49; (Alamy Stock Photo): 109; (James Mortimer): 38; (Robert Morris): 7. Paul Highnam: frontispiece, 2, 14, 27, 85, 105. Peter Curno: 20. Peter Draper: 9, 12. Richard Pollard: 113. Roger Dixon and Stefan Muthesius, *Victorian Architecture*, 1988: 117. Sheffield Local Studies Library: 124. Steven Cole: 23, 32, 44, 104. *The Survey of London* (vol. 18, 1937): 98. The Trustees of Haddon Hall: 6. Vaughan Hart: 50